KU-649-864

Contents

Illustrations

*(The following illustrations
appear between pages 96 and 97)*

The maps on pages vii–x are in ascending order of scale. The inset box in each indicates the area covered by the next map.

A CALABASH OF DIAMONDS

MARGARET LANE

A Calabash of Diamonds

AN AFRICAN TREASURE HUNT

THE REPRINT SOCIETY LONDON

FIRST PUBLISHED 1961

THIS EDITION PUBLISHED BY THE REPRINT SOCIETY LTD
BY ARRANGEMENT WITH WILLIAM HEINEMANN LTD., 1962

© MARGARET LANE 1961

To Jack, with love

PRINTED IN GREAT BRITAIN BY RICHARD CLAY AND COMPANY, LTD.,
BUNGAY, SUFFOLK

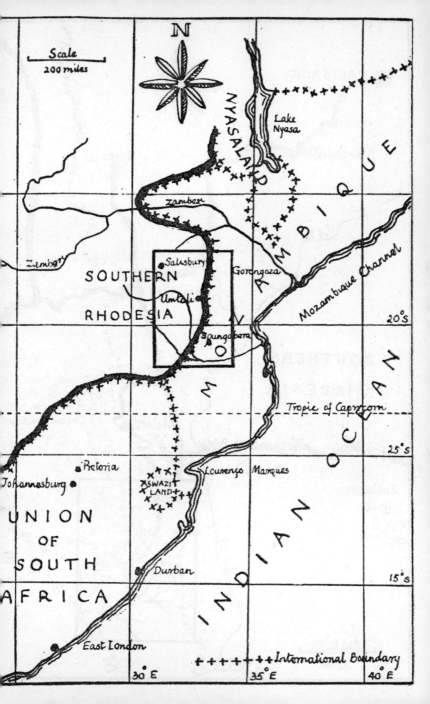

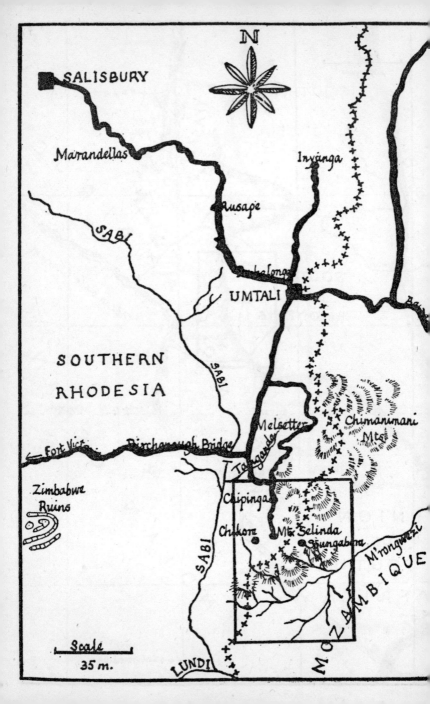

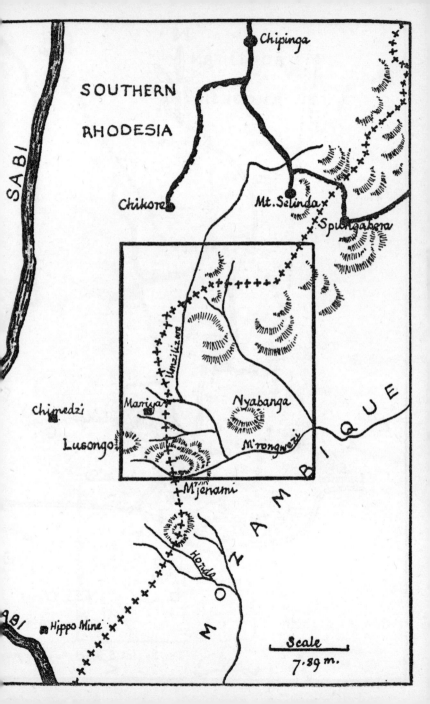

SOUTHERN

RHODESIA

SABI

Chipinga

Chikore

Mt. Selinda

Spungabera

Chimedzi

Mariya

Umzilizwe

Nyabanga

Lusongo

M'rongwezi

M'jenami

Hordze

Hippo Mine

MOÇAMBIQUE

Scale
7·89 m.

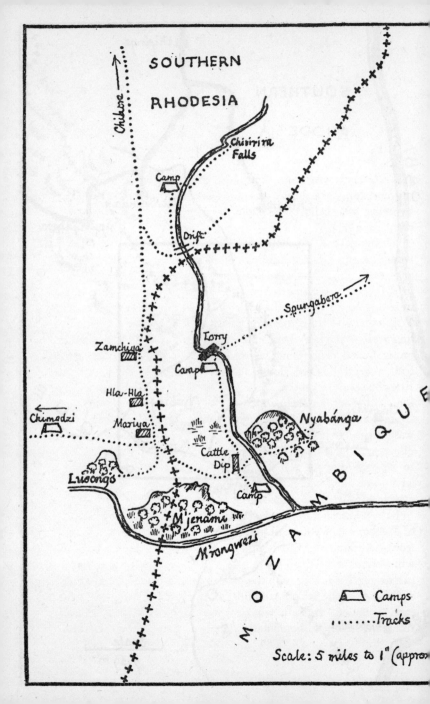

SOUTHERN

RHODESIA

Chibora →

Chiririra
Falls

Camp

Drift

Spungabera →

Zamchiya

Lorry

Camp

Hla-Hla

Chimodzi

Mariya

Nyabánga

Cattle
Dip

Lusongo

Camp

M'jenami

M'rongwezi

M O Z A M B I Q U E

△⃞ Camps
...... Tracks

Scale: 5 miles to 1" (approx

Russell's Narrative

A GOOD many years ago, long before we had met one another, my husband was told the story of a buried treasure, and given, by a man who believed he had not long to live, a written narrative, and a map.

This man was a solitary hard-bitten sort of adventurer, of whose origins I know nothing. His name was Samuel Russell, and at the time I speak of he was living on the island of Moorea in the South Seas, married to a Polynesian wife and making a modest living from vanilla and copra. Before the First World War he had been a prospector in various parts of Africa, travelling on foot and horseback in search of gold and other profitable minerals and penetrating far into undeveloped territories. He had worked up and down the eastern border of Southern Rhodesia and into the plains and hills of Mozambique, panning for gold in rivers and scratching up the earth, living off the country in the resourceful hand-to-mouth fashion at which he was adept. He had nearly died at one time of malaria and other diseases, and had left Africa, as he thought, for a while, intending to go back; but the war had intervened, and he had had other adventures, and was now too old and sick to believe he would ever return. He died, indeed, not long after.

Jack, whom I later married, had fallen in love with the island of Moorea in the course of an erratic and leisurely voyage home from Australia, and had bought a house on the beach, built of white coral, and a small copra plantation; and was living happily in that gentle paradise with the sense of unplanned life stretching endlessly ahead, which sanguine temperaments enjoy in their early twenties. Russell, who at that time was getting on for sixty, was his neighbour, and they spent much time together.

The friendship prospered, and some time before Jack gave up his life on the lagoon and came back to England, Russell, who had no son, and knew that he was now too old to finish the adventure, wrote for him all he remembered of the story and site of a buried treasure, one of the many under the soil of Africa, which he himself had failed to find, but which he firmly believed existed, guarded by powerful taboos and by the peculiar hazards of the country. He impressed on him the difficult nature of the search, and the necessity of secrecy. 'You're young,' he said. 'One day perhaps you will find yourself in Africa, and will be able to try your luck.' It seemed unlikely, but possible; and what young man is indifferent to the sort of adventure Russell appeared to offer? Jack accepted the written narrative, and a map roughly drawn on a scrap of paper. He put them away in a box and locked it, with the feeling that some day, somewhere, this esoteric knowledge might come in useful. He did not really believe he would ever search, but it was a satisfying thing to have under lock and key. The box eventually went back with him to England, where the papers lay undisturbed for thirty years.

Russell's narrative, which I have before me, soiled and frayed by much handling and by the red-brown dust of Mozambique which gets into everything, can be divided into three parts; and it will be easiest to consider these separately, since the narrative itself follows no plan and moves backwards and forwards in time, confusingly enough. There is the story of how Russell first came to hear of the treasure; his account of its nature and history so far as he was able to discover them; and his own determined but frustrated attempt to find it, which seems to have taken place (he is bad at dates) about the year 1910.

At that time he was one of a trio of prospectors, working in partnership and living by what they found, like innumerable other forgotten pioneers. The names of the other two were Bullock and McAlly. Of Bullock we know nothing beyond the fact that his initials were E. S., that he was known as Ned, and that he had a brother Bob who for a time was associated with the venture. Of McAlly, Russell recorded nothing but that he was 'a big New Zealander'. They were in that easternmost part of Southern Rhodesia where the Sabi, a huge river running almost directly north and south through sand-dunes and swamp, is joined by the Lundi at a point which touches the frontier of Mozambique. They were working slowly north, sometimes on one side of the border, sometimes on the other. (There is nothing, even today, in that wilderness of bush and rock and scrub-covered hills to show where Rhodesia ends and Portuguese East Africa, or Mozambique, to give it its Portuguese name, begins.) They were travelling on horseback and on foot, with African bearers and a number of pack animals, making camp wherever the ground looked promising for their purpose, and then moving on.

At an unnamed native village they were asked for medicine for a sick woman, and were surprised to find, lying in one of the thatched huts, a handsome Zulu girl of proud appearance, who was alone there among a strange people, nearly a thousand miles from home. Now this is not Zulu country: the people are called Vandau, and are an undistinguished branch of the Mashona tribe. Nevertheless in this particular area there is a fairly strong admixture of Zulu blood, due to a small migration in the nineteenth century, as we shall see presently; and this girl had come from far-away Natal with her father, apparently on a search for lost relations. She was now stranded, her father having died in this strange country, and was being nursed kindly enough by the local people, who recognized her quality and told the travellers that she was of noble birth, related to a chief. As pioneers they had a rough knowledge of medicine, and while they carried out their prospecting in this area Ned Bullock treated the girl as best he could, not yet aware of the nature of her malady. After a time she seemed to recover, and eventually he persuaded her to go with him, as his mistress.

She seems to have been a remarkable creature, dignified, gentle

and handsome, as many Zulu women are; she remained devoted
to Bullock until her death. None of the three men bothered with
her real name. At the first encounter they had nicknamed her
'the Countess' because of her air of breeding, and the Countess
she remained, accepting the change of name with perfect dignity.

Some time after this (I do not know how long) the Countess
confided to Bullock a Zulu secret, which she had learned before
her father's death when they had been living together among
the border tribes. Somewhere in the area, she did not know
precisely where, a great treasure was buried, in a place known to
the Zulu elders of the region. How it came to be there, and what
it was, was an involved story. It was proper that her father, as a
Zulu dignitary of high rank, should have been entrusted with
this knowledge, but the Countess's information was fragmentary,
picked up from scraps of the old men's conversation. Russell's
narrative contains a rough account of this story as he and
Bullock gradually pieced it together. He gives no details, but the
main facts correspond to the little that is certainly known from
Zulu history.

In 1837 a Zulu chief named Umgila, one of the many who
flourished precariously under Dingaan (murderer and successor
of the great Chaka), was engaged in a private war with his
brother, who disputed his right to the chieftainship. After a long
struggle Umgila was defeated and finally driven north out of
Zulu territory. He led his followers by degrees for about six
hundred miles, eventually settling among the Mashona people of
Gazaland, on the Longwegi River. Some say that he conquered
this peaceable branch of the Mashona, others that he came with
only a small body of men and a great number of women, widows
of his dead warriors. At all events he established himself there in
authority and his followers intermarried with the natives, pro-
ducing a mixed race who called themselves Mashangana. These
people were proud of their Zulu blood and aped Zulu customs,
but were, according to Russell, far inferior to their warlike
ancestors.

Umgila lived to a great age. The date of his death is not recorded, but Russell was certain it could not have been earlier than 1890. He died possessed of great riches, in cattle, gold, ivory and diamonds. The diamonds came from the Kimberley mines in Griqualand, which were opened in 1870 and developed their fabulous wealth under Cecil Rhodes. Native labour was drawn from many parts of Africa, and Umgila annually sent his quota of men. For many years large gangs of Mashangana would travel on foot the hundreds of miles to Kimberley, work for a spell of six months or a year and come back with their earnings and possessions packed in a small tin trunk which was carried on the head. In those early days it was easy for a native digger to conceal an uncut stone and bring it away, and Umgila made it a rule that each of his men should bring him at least one diamond. In this way, at some risk to his miners but no trouble to himself, he amassed a considerable treasure. He was already rich in ivory, and his wage-earning men brought him tribute in English gold; but the detail with which the Countess electrified her hearers was that he had died possessed of a fair-sized calabash of diamonds.

This, in accordance with Zulu custom, was buried with him, together with his weapons, his drinking vessels, and everything else of value that he owned. The site of the grave would be kept secret, and would also be sacred, a place of reverence and fear for several generations. Nevertheless, at this time there must still have been many of the older men of Zulu blood who knew where it was, and it was possible that the grave might still be marked by some observance. There would probably be a mound, with a planted tree on top, and on ceremonial occasions a pot of native beer would be carried to the place and left beneath the tree to propitiate his spirit.

Russell does not say whether the Countess originally told them this story with the idea of helping them to find Umgila's treasure. Most probably she did not; she was a Zulu and, like most Africans to this day, would regard the opening of a grave as the most dangerous impiety possible to commit, a desecration inviting terrible revenge. But she had cast in her lot with Bullock and was dependent on her new life, different in thought and habit from all she had known, and so, one supposes, was open to persuasion. She agreed to help them, and for many months, Russell says, of secret and patient inquiry they worked their way up and down Umgila's territory, ostensibly busy with nothing but mineral prospecting, but in reality searching for clues and information.

Their plan, at first, was to prepare the Countess for an expedition without them, since it would have been natural for her as a Zulu to ask to be shown the Chief's grave, to pray to his spirit and scatter a handful of earth. Also they well knew that she would have a better chance of gathering information if she were not accompanied by white men, always objects of suspicion, to whom no sacred thing may ever, in any circumstances, be shown. But by the time their plans were ready the Countess's malady, which they now knew to be consumption, took a turn for the worse, and she was too ill to travel.

Russell is vague about dates, but it seems that the partners set off on their search without her in 1910 or '11. Making their way through Rhodesian territory they crossed the Mozambique border at a point which Russell calls 'Mandhlami's kraal', struck south to the Longwegi River, and followed its course until they found, without much difficulty, the site of Umgila's deserted kraal, which was on the south bank and still identifiable. This was in the dry season, between March and October, when the rivers are low and for the most part easily forded. The kraal had been abandoned after the Chief's death, and was still not too thickly overgrown for them to be able to distinguish the floor of the principal hut, made, according to custom, of beaten ant-heap smeared with bullock's dung and blood, a mixture which dries almost to the hardness of cement. The huts had been built in straight lines in a square enclosure bordered with planted trees. The trees were now old and of a good size, forming three sides of the square, which was completed by the river. Even at this season the water was deep here, forming a long, beautiful and shady pool where Umgila's wives, 'the old queens', used to bathe.

Russell and Bullock had convinced themselves, from all they had learned of Zulu custom, that the Chief was probably buried under the floor of his hut, or in the courtyard surrounding it. He would be lying not more than six feet down, in a chamber roofed with wood and stones, perhaps lying on the bodies of the slaves who had dug the grave. Russell could not remember why they had been so much obsessed with the certainty of this idea, for the burial of a chief under his own hut, though common, was by no means invariable. The Countess had said only that he *might* be there; she had no positive knowledge. They accordingly made their camp beside the river and criss-crossed the floor of the hut and courtyard with trenches to a depth of about six feet, without result. It was not an encouraging dig, for, as he wrote, 'To us, accustomed to mining, it was quite obvious that the natural stratification of the alluvial pebble beds and formation beneath had never been interfered with.'

Their next attempt was made at the foot of a large tree at some distance from the Chief's hut, but still within the confines of the kraal. Here the grass had been carefully cleared, and in the roots of the tree stood a clay pot with the stale remains of sour-smelling native beer. These were promising signs, but when they had wasted a further day in digging the ground they learned from the local natives (who as always were never far away, uneasily watchful) that this had been a favourite sitting-place of the old Chief's, and was therefore a place for honouring his spirit. They next, rather desperately, dug up the whole kraal, which must have taken many days of hard labour, but found nothing for their pains but the grave of a woman, containing bones and some beads of an ancient pattern.

At this point, exasperated by the impossibility of getting the truth from any of the local natives, they inveigled the headman

of a near-by village to the kraal and strung him up to a branch
of Umgila's tree. This reckless action produced an important
clue, which at the time, however, they failed to profit by. When
the man had been hanging long enough to be near death, and
in a suitable state of terror, they offered to cut him down on
condition that he would tell them where Umgila was buried.
On being released, however, he was unable to tell them anything
coherent. All he could do was to point away to the north and
pour out a flood of choking speech in which one word was many
times repeated: 'kyabanga', a word which made no sense to any
of them. 'Fearing,' says Russell mildly, 'that perhaps we had
carried matters a bit too far, we let him go.' Clearly they had
not improved their chances with the natives.

A series of misfortunes now beset them which must have
convinced the onlookers that Umgila's spirit was moving towards revenge. The three men sickened at the same time with
malaria, and for a time could neither pursue their search nor
move on. Their resistance was low, for at this latter end of the
dry season the country was burned to a cinder and there were
no pumpkins or other fresh vegetables to be had, with which
they normally varied their meat diet. They were living wholly
on such meat as they could shoot, and the remains of dried
biltong that they carried with them. They were tormented by
thirst, and made matters worse by drinking great quantities of
the river water, which gave them dysentery and weakened them
still further. (They later learned that the local natives did not
drink this water, but fetched every drop from a stream two
miles farther north; but by the time they discovered this the
damage was done.) Their own natives, too, were suffering from
the water, and in a state of terror at being involved in the
digging up of graves. The three men, sick as they were, had to
take it in turn to watch them night and day, for it was only too
evident that at the slightest relaxation of discipline they would
down tools and disappear into the bush, leaving them with no
choice but to abandon their gear. This decided them to pull out

of the unwholesome area while they still had the strength, and to return after the long rains, when conditions might be improved and their own health better.

Accordingly they set out, as soon as they could, in a northerly direction, to climb by degrees into wooded and hilly country, where the air is cool at night and the mosquitoes are fewer. No sooner did they leave Umgila's neighbourhood, however, than a new trouble broke out among their carriers. They complained that the trail was 'heavy' and showed a great unwillingness to follow it, throwing down their packs, demanding rest, and proposing trails at random in other directions. The three pushed on, however, disregarding the protests of the natives as only men can who carry rifles; and before long were in the high veldt, making slow progress across a series of hills and valleys towards the Rhodesian border.

It was on this part of the trail, Russell says, that he overheard the word *kyabanga* in the conversation of two of his carriers, but, being languid with malaria, at the time attached no great importance to it. They fell silent in any case as soon as they noticed he was near. He and the Bullock brothers were by this time so 'saturated with malaria' that they had neither heart nor energy for anything new, and were concentrating on getting alive and without further mishap out of this part of the country. It was not until much later (he does not say when or where) that Russell fell in with an old Zulu bullock-driver who had spent some time in Umgila's country, and who innocently told him, when asked, that the word *kyabanga* did not *mean* anything, so far as he knew, but was the name of a hill where a great chief was buried. From his description it seemed that the trail which Russell had taken into the high veldt must have passed very near this hill, which would therefore be only a few miles away from Umgila's old kraal, in a north-easterly direction. This was important news, but it had come too late. The partners were in no condition to continue the search; their money had run out, and they would have to recover financially as well as physically before they could hope to return to Mozambique. They decided to break up their partnership for a time, always intending, later, to renew the search; but this was not to be. Ned Bullock went off to Gadzema to the Grant mine, taking the Countess with him, and it was not long before she died of tuber-culosis in Hartley hospital, and so passes out of our story. McAlly had some time before this gone off to Nigeria to look for tin, and was never heard of again. Bob Bullock, being married, decided that he must have nothing more to do with risky adventures; he settled down in Penhalonga near Umtali. Before anything further could be done, the 1914 war had broken out, and this made a gap of several years in which Ned Bullock and Russell were both away from Africa. Ned Bullock died of shell-shock after the war, and it seems that Russell himself never found money or opportunity to return. How he came to end his days in the Pacific, living at ease with a handsome Tahitian wife, I do not know; but as a final scene it fits well enough with his tough and at the same time easy-going character.

2

The Cover Story

THIS, then, was the story which was first told to me ten years ago, as a curious footnote to one of Jack's occasional tales of the South Seas. He never dwells on personal reminiscence, and has an economical, half diffident way of bringing out, when pressed, the most surprising and recondite information. It was so with this story of Russell and the African treasure. We had been married a number of years and it had never been mentioned; whole areas of chequered life lay between that period and this; and now the box was unearthed and Russell's map and narrative dropped in my lap almost with an air of astonishment at my interest. We read it together, not stopping to disentangle the confused threads but swallowing it whole—the old Chief in his grave, the Countess, the pioneers, the uneasy natives, and at the heart of it, hidden in the dark of an airless cavity among ivory and bones, the calabash of diamonds. How big was a calabash, I wanted to know? They varied; they were commonly used for fetching and ladling water, and were carried on the head. As big as this? Or that? One couldn't tell. At all events a calabash was a notable thing to have filled with uncut stones.

We brooded luxuriously on the story, never for a moment seeing it as in any way connected with ourselves, but enjoying it for its own sake. It was simply a richly romantic thing to possess and dwell upon. If only Jack could have gone in Russell's life-time, we said, staring at one another. If only we knew some adventurous young man who had none of our ties and pre-occupations, and could embrace the adventure. We gazed at the map again—such a hopelessly scant little scrawl, yet, somehow, authentic—and turned once more to the closely written pages. 'To sum the thing up,' Russell had written, towards the end, 'the evidence for the existence of the treasure is, for one who is as well acquainted with African customs and languages as I am, overwhelming. What then are the chances of successfully locating the francs?* In this connection it must be remembered that the natives of the locality, whilst by no means hostile, would not respond to direct inquiry even if they knew anything. . . . The plan of action must be decided on the spot. My opinion is that there is an even chance of success for a man of the right sort, who is out for an adventure anyhow, and is patient and ob-servant. . . . Local information should be sought for the best route to take as the tracks may be improved since my time. Best to take out a mining licence in P.E.A.,† and then there is no kick coming and no suspicion. The real object should, it goes without saying, be kept dead secret. Beware especially of Native Com-missioners and their spies.' It did not sound as though it had anything to do with us, but we spent some pleasant evenings

* Treasure, loot.   † Portuguese East Africa.

wishing that it had. It seemed sad to let such a secret wither unused. Russell and Bullock were both dead; McAlly had disappeared years ago; it was unlikely that he could still be alive. Of Bob Bullock, the brother, Russell knew only that he had settled in Penhalonga, and if alive could 'give some information that may help, as he has, I believe, my diary of the trip; anyhow he knows the country and can give valuable advice. So far as I am aware the rest of the world knows nothing.'

I think our feeling at this time, apart from sheer pleasure in possessing such a story, was regret that there was no younger, more adventurous man to whom we could confide it. It was not a secret to be lightly given away, for, quite apart from the hazard of the thing and the complications that sprang up thick as briars as we discussed it, Russell had bequeathed this information with great seriousness, frankly weighing the chances, as one might bequeath an attractive but highly dubious investment. It was a nice present to give a younger brother, if we had had one; but we had not; and we finally concluded that the only person whom we could remotely imagine undertaking the search was Jack's nephew, Peter Cameron.

Some time passed before we were able to tell him anything. I think at the time he was still in West Africa or the Solomon Islands, pursuing a modest but promising career in the Colonial Service. He had had an adventurous war, had made some enterprising journeys in different parts of the world, and was regarded by us as tough, intelligent, and in certain perfectly congenial and unimportant respects, slightly dotty. He was thirty years old and physically strong, and we could just imagine him setting off on his own one day to look for Umgila's treasure.

We told him the story under promise of secrecy on one of his leaves, and found that we had not been wrong in supposing that he would be stirred by it. He yearned over it, as we had done, and with the same regret. How could he raise the money for such a venture? Besides, he was newly married, and had his career to consider. We observed with regret that Peter was settling down. Still, we spent an enjoyable evening with Russell's map and an atlas, in that intoxicating sort of discussion which the very notion of difficult travel induces; and parted for the night in an atmosphere of conspiracy and blood-brotherhood, soothed by the reflection that if things were different, and life more as it ought to be, we three would have been off to Africa in the morning.

As it was, things being as they are and life what it is, the map and the narrative were put away again and given no further thought for another eight years.

How it came about that in the winter of 1958 we began to think of the possibility of going to Africa ourselves, I am no longer clear. We had been unsettled and bemused by a journey to the Far East the year before, and were thirsting to try some new continent that neither of us had seen. Except that Jack had spent some weeks with Alec Waugh in Tangier, we had neither of us so much as set foot in Africa; and the more we considered this, the more our thoughts turned to Mozambique, and the unimaginable territory of which we knew nothing beyond the spidery lines of Russell's map. The thing, I believe, that most provoked and stimulated us was our ignorance. For all we knew, the treasure might have been discovered years ago; Jack remembered that Russell had said, in discussing this possibility, that some time in the nineteen-twenties a mysterious quantity of uncut diamonds had appeared on the market, which nobody could account for, and which had made him wonder. Then, supposing that it was still there, how did one set about searching for such a thing? We had no idea what the country was like, beyond that, from Russell's description, we assumed that it was difficult. We had only the haziest idea of where it was. We did not know how to get there, or what would be the best proceeding when one arrived. What we should need, if ever we decided to go, was good advice, and this, because of the necessity of secrecy, was clearly the one essential we could not have.

The more we thought of it, the more tantalizing the whole thing became, finally resolving itself into a single question . . . why should we not try? If we did not go, it was more than unlikely that anyone ever would, for so far as we knew there was no European alive who had heard of the treasure but Peter and ourselves. Perhaps it was already too late. It was more than forty years since Russell had made his attempt, and there was no knowing whether any of his clues were still valid, or the places recognizable. If we did not go soon we should never go, for it was not the sort of adventure for late middle-age. In any case, was it the kind of enterprise in which we *ought* to be involved? I am afraid we brushed this consideration aside. The lure of treasure is too strong for any but characters more disciplined than ours.

We began to study atlases and bought a large-scale map of Southern Africa. This, to our surprise, told us almost nothing. We could see the Sabi River running like a strong artery down Rhodesia, and the point at which, among fringes of swamp, the Lundi joined it; but as soon as the eye travelled farther east, into Mozambique, it lost itself in a desert of blank paper. We applied to several of those beautiful map shops whose windows, baited with terrestrial globes and Ordnance Survey maps in leather cases, delay one so pleasantly in walking about London; but none of them, it seemed, could furnish us with a map of Mozambique. Faintly exasperated by this apparent inefficiency, we went next to the library of the Royal Geographical Society, and here it was borne in upon us for the first time that details of this part of the Portuguese hinterland were perhaps not to be found on any map. Maps of Rhodesia turned blank and pale as soon as they came to the border; the Portuguese had mapped the developed coastal area with thoroughness, and had left the remote interior alone. In some maps, a network of rivers appeared, unnamed. In others, a few names were to be found, but the rivers were unaccountably running in other directions. In no two maps did the names of the rivers agree. Gingerly, and assuming innocuous geographical expressions, we approached the Portuguese Embassy, and after parrying a great many courteously inquisitive questions were told that they had no maps of this area at present. The proper department would have them in Lisbon, no doubt. They could be sent for. We gratefully made arrangements for this to be done, but days and weeks passed and nothing came.

We now realized with some alarm that if we were to have any hope of keeping our motive secret we had got to invent a plausible cover story. People who contemplate making an African journey are invariably questioned, usually with goodwill, sometimes with a curiosity that is very like suspicion. Was there a political motive behind our idea? Why were we interested in this particular territory? We had been told that the Portuguese are inclined to be sensitive about their African colonies. They welcome tourists to Beira, to the Gorongoza Game Reserve and to the Indian Ocean resorts along the coast; but they do not care to have foreigners poking about and going where they choose. We were several times asked at the Embassy, was it our intention to write articles? We gathered the impression that, if this had been our aim, it would have met with skilled discouragement.

Nor was it any use, we found, explaining ourselves by saying we were going on safari. A very few inquiries among people who had indulged in this costly pastime convinced us that if this had been so, we should never have given a thought to this part of the map. We should be going, of course, to Kenya or Tanganyika, hiring American cars and camping equipment and taking a White Hunter. That was what everybody did. That was the way to shoot game, with gun or camera. It cost a good deal, of course, but you had marvellous servants and fingerbowls at dinner. It had been brought to a fine art and was very comfortable. Nobody, said the few who knew anything about it, went down to the area we were vaguely indicating on the map. Wasn't it a malarial and tsetse-fly area? Hadn't the game been systematically shot out by the Rhodesian Government, and wasn't it in any case primitive and nasty? We found that the best reply was to ask for guidance, and to receive with patience a good deal of information about parts of Africa we did not want to go to.

The need for a cover story became urgent, for without one we plainly saw we should get nowhere, or at least not to the places we wished to see. It could be eccentric, but it had got to be innocuous, and sufficiently convincing to allay suspicion. This was not easy, and when we had invented our tale we were tormented by the doubt that between us we ought to have been able to think of a better. However, we could not. It had got to have some element of truth in it, to account for our searching, and we finally hit on the simple expedient of using the topographical part of Russell's story, and changing Russell himself into my uncle.

Now, my mother had had a strange and ne'er-do-well step-uncle, who had attracted her greatly as a child, and with whose shady adventures she had long ago regaled me. He had been in prison once, which was a great scandal, and had wandered about the world in an undesirable way, and had been eventually killed, I believe, in the South African War. I remember little about him beyond the fact that, on the rare occasions when he came home to roost, he used to stand on his head to amuse my mother, and that when he did this a gold sovereign always rolled out of his pocket. This was attractive; also the fact that he was much disapproved of in the family for his boon companions, with whom he used to sing in harmony when he came home late, taking off his shoes to cross the shadows in the street, as though they had been streams. There was also a dark suggestion that there had been something irregular even about his death; that he had been shot for desertion or some other misdemeanour, instead of in the proper manner, facing the Boers. My mother had remembered him fondly, with indulgence for his faults, and it seemed quite fitting that we should change him into the brother she had never had, and give him the adventures that had befallen Russell.

This, then, was the story with which we armed ourselves. My mother had had a favourite brother who had been an adventurer. He had spent some years pioneering in Southern Africa, and had written my mother a series of interesting letters. These letters, with some of his old diaries of travel, had come to me after her death; and since my uncle had been a character, and the letters had a period interest and were amusing, I had been taken with the notion of following up some of his travels and writing an account of him. It was, in short, a pious task that I had set myself; one which we hoped no one was likely to investigate too closely.

This step taken, and a copy of Russell's narrative made and his map traced, we turned our attention to other practical matters. It was hard to know where to begin. Our ignorance of Africa was so complete that merely to look at the map brought on a feeling of almost panic helplessness. We were beginning to see that the journey we had in mind was less likely to be a trip than an expedition, and we had no idea of equipping an expedition, nor of what we should need, nor how we should set about it. Advice was what we must have, and fortified by my uncle and his imaginary letters we cast about for the best way of obtaining it.

It happened that Jack had years ago known a handsome and resourceful Austrian who at one period of his life had earned his living in Africa as a White Hunter. A White Hunter can be roughly defined as a man skilled in the ways of game and methods of hunting it, who for a high fee professionally takes charge of safaris, organizes the camping arrangements, directs the native servants, and provides his clients with sport and excitement in conditions of reasonable safety. It would, of course, be invaluable for us to be accompanied by such a man, but then there was the difficult question, what should we tell him? He would be professionally interested in big game, and there might be little or none in our special area. He would be the greatest help in finding our way about, for he would presumably have some knowledge of native languages, but how could we take him with us without telling him the whole story? We knew enough of the law of treasure trove to be pretty certain that if ever we found the treasure, whatever we did with it was bound to be illegal. The laws relating to buried treasure vary slightly from country to country, but they have one attribute in common, that they are always unfavourable and discouraging to the trover. In most countries you must declare your findings immediately to the police and hand over the whole treasure to the government. This applies, with variations, even to treasure found on land owned by yourself, and is unqualified in respect of treasure in foreign territory. Any attempt to remove and keep such treasure would be not only difficult, but a penal offence, and we had glanced obliquely at the possibility that, if we should try to smuggle anything out of Mozambique (let alone what we did with it afterwards), we might well end up inside a Portuguese prison. In the Union of South Africa the possession of an undeclared uncut diamond is in itself illegal; and indeed the laws relating to diamonds all over the world are uniformly punitive and disagreeable.

It could therefore be only with the greatest caution that we could think of taking a partner in our enterprise. It would be better to have none: but how far should we get without one, with our lack of native languages, our total ignorance? In the end we wrote guardedly to our Austrian, knowing him to have been an adventurous man in his youth, and asked him whether he would be interested in joining us on a little expedition, and if so, what was likely to be the cost? He replied, amiably enough, that he probably could manage it, though he did not know the part of Africa we mentioned, nor its languages, and had never heard that it was remarkable for game. He strongly recommended Kenya or Tanganyika. He also added, considerately, that he supposed we knew that the fees of a White Hunter for two months (the period we had guessed at) would be extremely high, even if we enlisted one on the spot, and that in his case there would be the additional expense, two hundred pounds or more, of a first-class return air fare between Mozambique and Austria. He suggested as an economical alternative that we should apply to a cousin of his, who was a travel and safari agent in Salisbury, Southern Rhodesia, and who would, he was sure, be able to fit us out with all we needed, and who would no doubt be able to provide us with native servants who would act as interpreters and who would know some English. In any case he thought it a good idea that we should learn some Portuguese, and he sent us his blessing.

We were grateful for this advice though we found it discouraging, for the more we learned the more obvious it became that we could not undertake the expedition alone. I think my chief apprehension was that Jack, who has been known to break a leg in the most improbable circumstances, would damage himself, or get ill, or be bitten by a snake, and how should I cope with this emergency, possibly miles out in the bush, with no one to turn to but strange and perhaps disgruntled African servants? We needed at least a second man, but a strange White Hunter, for various reasons, was out of the question. He would formidably send up the cost, and how could we know, starting blind, that we could trust him? Supposing he downed tools when the moment of truth arrived, and refused to have anything further to do with it? Supposing we were successful in our search, and he judged it more prudent or profitable to report us to the authorities? Supposing he just went off with the swag, leaving us alone in the jungle, secure in the knowledge that there was nothing whatever that we could do about it? It did not bear thinking of.

Our thoughts at this point turned again to Peter Cameron. He had left the Colonial Service some years ago and was now settled with a growing family, farming in Gloucestershire. True, he would not know any of the native languages of our part of

Africa, but he was tough, resourceful, and, what was even more important, one of us. We made a pretext for fetching him up to London, and rather timidly outlined our scatter-brained idea. To our pleased surprise (for by this time we were so conscious of the daydream nature of the enterprise that we expected him to laugh at it) he responded at once, and before we knew what had happened we were all three of us on the floor again with maps, all talking together, thumbing through Russell's narrative, calculating wet and dry seasons, and whether Peter could safely leave the hay to his foreman, if he were back for the harvest. I remember that Peter's farming experience, which was not yet very extensive, fortified us extremely. He was used to driving a Land Rover, and would, he said, go to Solihull for the three days' engineering course, in which they taught one to drive down chasms and through rivers and mud, and to take the engine to pieces efficiently afterwards. He gave us the idea, too, that we might be able to buy some sort of detector, which would give us a clue to gold hidden underground, and so save a great deal of trouble. Mine-detectors had been used with success in the war and were easy to carry, and Peter himself had a similar appliance which he used on his cows, and which told him whenever they had swallowed nails or had fencing wire in their stomachs.

This seemed an idea worth following, and so, while Peter undertook to discover whether the War Office had detailed maps of our territory, and Jack investigated the laws of treasure trove with a discreet legal acquaintance, I went off in simple hope to South Kensington, to the Geological Museum, to try and get information about gold-detectors. We were not so sanguine as to suppose that a machine existed for detecting buried diamonds, but there *had* been a paragraph in *The Times* about a man who claimed to have invented an electric divining-rod which detected practically all metals, to say nothing of rubber and other uninteresting substances; and Russell had said that Umgila's hoard had included a good deal of gold, which might give us the signal we needed. The only difficulty was, what reason could I give for desiring this information? The keepers of departments in museums are usually helpful, and will take trouble to satisfy serious inquiries; but they like to know what the information is for, and why you want it. On the way to the museum I made up another story.

My nephew, I told the presence behind the desk, had a small farm, on which ancient coins of no great value had been occasionally turned up by the plough. This had given him the idea (we exchanged indulgent smiles) that he might one day with luck uncover a hoard, and it was my intention to give him a modest metal-detector as a birthday present. Did such things exist? It must of course be portable, and preferably not expensive. I entertained, I said, no extravagant hopes that he would ever be successful, but it was an interesting hobby and I wished to contribute to it. The presence shook his head. He knew of no device, he said, which reacted electrically to non-ferrous metals. Iron was easy, the army mine-detector was the thing for that, but copper and gold, that was a different matter. Archaeologists would all be glad of a treasure-detector, and the Americans were said to be doing research on these lines; but so far nothing had been produced, and he was of the opinion that if anything so specialized were ever perfected it would be proportionately expensive. He roamed about over his bookshelves and searched for information in several volumes. They were full of helpful advice about iron, but had nothing to say about searching for Roman coins. The only method, he said, was to remove the earth skin by skin like an archaeologist, and this was clearly no pastime to suggest to a busy farmer.

What about dowsing? I asked. This was a practice I knew nothing about from experience, but had so often been told by believers that it worked, and was an unpredictable gift possessed by many, that I would like to know what geologists thought about it. Would it be worth trying our luck with a hazel-twig, just in case? The expert shook his head again and smiled.

Official science, he said, took no cognisance of dowsing. There was a society of dowsers in existence (he wrote down its address) and he would not be prepared to say that there was nothing in it; but his own view was that successful dowsers were also, whether they admitted it or not, good amateur geologists, who knew from the geological formation where water was most likely to be found, and therefore frequently found it. If the dowsers' society could supply a diviner who specialized in copper or gold, it would be interesting to let him walk over the fields in question. He himself, however, would be bound to regard the experiment as being roughly on the same level as fortune-telling. I left him with a private resolve that I would try out a hazel-twig myself when I had the opportunity; but I could not see us taking a dowser to Africa.

3

We Set Out

THE expedition now began to take shape; we planned to leave England at the end of April. We had sought advice from one or two acquaintances who had had experience of Africa, and now had a fair idea of what we needed and what we could afford. Our preparations were still based on guesswork, for the curious anomaly persisted that nobody could tell us anything about the terrain. Nobody, it seemed, knew anything about the Mozambique side of the Southern Rhodesian border, and our Portuguese advice was to leave that part of the country alone, as being of no interest. The official Rhodesian handbooks we consulted spoke always optimistically (and to us ominously) of 'development'. The country was being opened up: millions of pounds were to be spent on this or that; roads and schools and hospitals were mentioned; the climate was recommended. We began to fear that when we arrived, with all the impedimenta of an expedition, we should find ourselves perhaps in a garden suburb, with Umgila sealed off under an asphalt playground. This would be the worst blow of all, and so disgusting a possibility that we refused to consider it. Besides, in spite of the handbooks, there was still the enigmatic blankness of the maps and the total absence of first-hand information. There was nothing to do but to prepare ourselves for the sort of country Russell had described, and to hope that the intervening years had not brought about some ludicrous transformation.

Hearing that we planned to go where there might be no roads to speak of and that the country was said to be swampy, the Land Rover Company recommended two long-wheel-base vehicles equipped with a powerful winch and hauling gear, so that whichever got into difficulties could be pulled out by the other. We three could travel in one and our native driver and African servants in the other; vehicles of this type would be long enough to sleep in. On the other hand, a distinguished and kindly explorer whom we questioned was of the opinion that we were never likely to be out of reach of an hotel, or at least a rest camp. We could go in hired American cars and do the thing comfortably. He added, however, that this was merely his view of the probability; he had never been in that part of Africa and did not know the country.

The agent at Salisbury, written to at length, was more practical. He had no information about the Portuguese territory, but judging by the Sabi River area on the Rhodesian side advised us to take a short-base Land Rover and a four-ton diesel lorry, and undertook to buy these second-hand to save expense. He would provide tents and camping equipment, including a refrigerator, and basic supplies sufficient for two months. As to African servants, the smallest number he thought we could manage with was three, and these he would have waiting for us in Salisbury. They would be of unimpeachable character and would speak English. He did not think we would need the picks and shovels we had disingenuously mentioned as an essential part

B

of the Land Rover's equipment. He thought it more important
to have a snake-bite outfit.

All this was beginning to sound luxurious but he made it clear
that, by safari standards, our ideas were humble. Did we really
not wish for a White Hunter? An extra bearer, perhaps, to
carry the guns? An African driver? We replied that we would
do the driving ourselves and that one of us at least would have
some practical knowledge of the motors. Unlike most expeditions, ours was to be a self-supporting venture. We were not
making a film, we were not backed by a petrol company or any
other advertiser, and we were not rich. The correspondence
made us vaguely uneasy.

As a concession to me, who longed for the new experience of
a south-bound voyage, it was settled that Jack and I should
travel to Cape Town by sea, and that Peter, leaving a fortnight
later, should fly to Salisbury. There we would spend a few days
fitting out, buying boots and bush shirts and anything else we
needed. We would have time on the voyage to make lists of
necessities, to master the contents of a Portuguese phrase book,
and think of a great many answers to awkward questions.

These hypothetical questions, and indeed the whole idea of
our undertaking, retreated at once into realms of the utmost
absurdity from the moment when we first set foot in the ship.
In our neat cabin, surrounded by flowers and potted plants from
indulgent friends, it became impossible to believe that we were
other than we seemed—a staid couple setting off for a routine
holiday in South Africa. As the ship moved at majestic speed
through waters that we knew so well, the discouraging observa-
tions of the experienced rang in our ears and made the whole
thing ridiculous. 'Why on earth do you want to go to South
Africa? Have you got relations there, or what? I suppose you
know that you're going at the wrong time of year? It's the
winter there, of course. Terribly boring country, from all
accounts. And the people! You'll have to keep your mouths
shut on the colour question. . . .' I went to bed before we were

out of the Solent, and for a day and a night, without waking or eating, slept.

After that, though I was wide awake and tried to apprehend it, the life of the ship persisted as a dream. We were enclosed in a world of solid business, of sober sensible citizens borne about the world on expense accounts, pursuing their prosperous affairs. We were beset by deck games and after-dinner dances, by fancy dress and competitions, by weirdly monotonous food and weak tea, by polite conversation and cocktail parties. We lay fallow in deck chairs, eating sun and wind, swam doggedly in the ship's indoor pool for hours, laboured in the gymnasium, and walked barefoot many wind-blown miles a day in an effort to lose our London softness and harden our muscles.

The relief of solitude first returned when we docked at Las Palmas. Most of the passengers left the ship here; they were going for pleasure, for holidays and honeymoons, the victims of shipping lines and travel agencies. We saw them at the rail in the first light, carrying their coats and rugs, looking dubiously at this shore of metallic barrenness, at the dusty palms in the municipal gardens, rattling their sabres in the persistent wind. I had picked up a travel folder the day before, and had read that it was 'not surprising that the Canary Islands conjure up thoughts of Elysium'. Las Palmas is a stony, treeless island, rising abruptly to shaly-looking hills and to mountains covered with artificial snow. There is something wrong about this snow; there is too much of it, and the whiteness is unconvincing. It is in fact a disagreeable mineral deposit. The Irish steward whom we questioned said it was a sad place, overcast with cloud whenever he had seen it, and always with this dusty wind blowing. Its real business, he said, was bunkering ships, and for his own part he never bothered to go ashore; there was more gaiety in Belfast.

With Las Palmas mercifully left behind, and before us long days of ocean, wind and sun—for the sun appeared in splendour when the island was out of sight and flying-fish began to spray out of the bow wave like sequins—we brooded, with an ever-growing sense of unreality, on the adventure before us. Supposing we found the diamonds, what happened next? It might be possible to get them out of Africa without suspicion if we moved quickly, but once in Europe we might find we had made a noose for our own necks. Which of us would smuggle them, and how? How quickly would news of the dig follow us from Africa? What hope had we of keeping a search secret? We asked each other these questions between long intervals of silence, sitting with our Portuguese grammars in our laps and the empty southern ocean streaming by. It seemed at least prudent to have a series of signals which could be sent home in an emergency; we supposed that this amenity would be allowed even in a cell, and worked out a sentence in Portuguese which we hoped would mean 'I wish to send a telegram to my mother'. We then devised a number of code messages, all apparently innocuous and filial, with corresponding meanings to cover the most disagreeable circumstances we could think of. 'Please reassure Mother all well' implied 'Make immediate inquiries through diplomatic channels', and so on. It seemed unlikely that we would not be allowed to make this simple communication even under arrest, and we learned the sentences by heart with some earnestness, and wrote out the code to be posted in Cape Town to a resourceful friend in London.

That done, the voyage became once more a trance of idleness, through which we passed with empty minds, believing nothing. We became tourists, and innocent, murmuring with surprise at the cold and drizzle of Cape Town, at the primitive discomforts of the South African train, the empty lunar landscape, the depressing towns, the bad food and the grit which deepened the long monotony of the land journey. But we ran into Salisbury at last, in a sunlit air so clear that it seemed to belong to the beginning of the world, and were greeted by a handsome man of stupendous height who proved to be our Austrian's cousin and our agent. Everything was briskly and competently done; we were shepherded into a brand-new station wagon and driven through shining streets to our hotel, where Peter was waiting for us, signalling with his eyebrows that something incalculable had happened. It had indeed. Our travel agent had become uneasy about the expedition; he did not like, he said—he put it more politely—to send three innocents like ourselves alone into the bush. He had got us the three best Africans he could, but was not happy about their ability to get us out of any unforeseen trouble. We did not speak any native language, and the *munts*— this was the first time we heard the contemptuous Afrikaans word for any African—were only *munts* and therefore not intelligent. So he had decided, he said, to send his son along with us. He was used to the bush, he knew how to handle natives. He was a good shot, and being keen on game would come for the fun of it, since he was luckily due for a month's leave and had nothing to do. Leave . . .? We exchanged apprehensive glances and held our breath. The next instant we were shaking hands with a young and handsome man, again of prodigious height, clad in the khaki uniform of a Rhodesian policeman.

Michael was six feet five, in military leggings, with cartridges round his waist and a broad-brimmed hat with a strip of leopard-skin round it. He was so impressive in appearance as to be disconcerting; he looked like the handsome star of an early Western, and seemed not wholly unconscious of this impression. When we had met his two younger brothers, who were the same size as himself and their father, we began to get used to it; but it was unnerving, even in the hotel bar, to find ourselves in such conspicuous company.

At the first possible moment we shut ourselves in Peter's bedroom and tried to think what in heaven's name we should do. We had expressed our gratitude for the new arrangement, which clearly offered practical advantages; but if we had rejected the idea of a White Hunter as too dangerous, what were we to do with a policeman? The uneasy thought even crossed our minds that he might have been wished on us by unseen powers. Our expedition was eccentric; it did not carry conviction; we were suspected of having a political motive and were to be kept under surveillance. If a watch were to be set on our proceedings, what more convenient device could authority employ than this young officer, sent in the harmless guise of helper and friend? We considered these ideas with strong misgiving: it might be so, but there was nothing we could do about it. Besides—though this was an impression, not an argument—Michael looked far too open and naïve to be a spy. If he were one, we could not believe that he would be much good at it.

Still, this left us with the problem almost as intractable, for if ever we succeeded in finding Umgila's grave, the moment would come when we should want to dig, and this was something which we should have to explain. Such a proceeding could not be accounted for by my uncle, nor by anything, in the last resort, but the truth; and how would this sort of truth appear to an officer of police, whose duty would be to prevent such illegal action, or, if he could not prevent it, to report it? We argued round and round this theme late into the night, and arrived at several provisional conclusions. First, it would be impossible to reject Michael without giving offence and laying ourselves open to suspicion. Secondly, since he spoke Shona, the prevalent native language of those parts, and presumably had experience of life in the bush, he would be of infinite help to us in finding our way, and obtaining (if we could disguise our reasons for wanting it) information. Then, of the three African servants who were now under contract, two were intimately known to him. John, a Zulu (we pricked up our ears at this), was his own batman, and Shorty, the camp boy, had been employed for several years in his father's stables. Only the cook, a Portuguese African, was an unknown quantity, and we felt that in dealing with all of them Michael's presence and authority would be invaluable. Besides, it was only too possible that we would never find the place we were looking for, and in that case there would be no occasion for enlightening him. If we did find it, of course he would have to be told, but we would not deal with that difficulty before we came to it. These things decided, we all felt a certain relief that he was going with us, though Peter's expression, I think, was more speculative than ours. Admitting every argument and seeing no alternative, he was yet privately convinced from the beginning that we should do better alone.

We now had to face some discussions with Michael's father, who naturally felt that the point had been reached when he ought to have a clearer idea of where we were going and what we were about, since we might easily, fools that we were, get into some difficulty for which he, professionally involved, would feel responsible. It became plain, as we talked, that this was his basic reason for sending Michael, and we gradually relaxed the suspicion that there was anything more than that behind the arrangement. Still, it was hard to convince him that our plans were sensible, since we were vague about our direction and vaguer still about the time we should need. He accepted my pious concern with my uncle's journey but thought it a pity, since it might easily take us, he said, into tedious country, where there might be no roads and where petrol supplies would be difficult. Much better, he thought, to concentrate on those parts of Southern Rhodesia which were known to be beautiful, where camping was easy and small game still relatively plentiful; or to go straight down to the Sabi and look for crocodile; or, if we were really determined to go into Portuguese East, to go in on the excellent Beira road and visit Gorongoza. He was a hunter himself, full of alarming stories of bush and game, and it was obvious that he thought our ideas both hare-brained and puny. He turned with a sigh to the question of guns and permits—so many rounds of this, so many of that—and, as a tolerant after-thought, some medical equipment. The one item which brought his private amusement to the surface was the pick, shovel and

crowbar that we kept insisting on, and which he waved aside
as quite superfluous. What were we afraid of? he wanted to
know. If we kept to the good roads there would be nothing
to worry us. If we went in the bush, the ground at this season
was dry. Nevertheless, when Peter put on his obstinate expression and said that he never went out in a Land Rover without
them, even in England, he shrugged his shoulders and said they
could be provided. (What was, in fact, thrown in at the last
moment was a square-ended shovel and a mattock, with neither
pick nor crowbar; but this we did not discover until later, when
we were in the process of learning how vital it is to make a personal check of all equipment.)

One prudent decision, at least, came out of these colloquies,
which were chiefly concerned with blankets, paraffin, water-bags,
bully-beef, cornflakes, tinned butter and the like – that we would
be wise to go into Mozambique at once, crossing the border at
an official frontier post and having our passports stamped in the
proper manner. This, we privately decided, was a sound precaution, even though we should have to come back into Rhodesia
by the same road and proceed south later. At the point at which
we guessed we should want to cross there was not a frontier
post for many miles, and we thought it unwise to make our first
entry in so ambiguous a manner, when we might be stopped and
questioned and would not be able to show any Portuguese
authority. If we went first to Gorongoza, which was a thing that
tourists did and which everyone understood, this would give
some colour, perhaps, to our presence later in other parts of the
territory, where tourists were never seen and had no reason to go.
We might, judging from Russell's map, find it necessary to cross
the border several times, and since there appeared to be no roads
to speak of, no towns and certainly no frontier posts in this
area, such activity, with unstamped papers, might lead to trouble.

Accordingly, with the full approval of Michael's father, who
had at last found something rational to deal with, we decided
to go straight to Gorongoza, which could be reached in two

days' driving on a good road from Salisbury. We three would go alone in the Land Rover, without either Michael or the lorry, since we should spend the first night in an hotel at Umtali and the following three in Gorongoza itself, where there was an up-to-date rest camp in the game reserve. Michael would meanwhile see the lorry packed and would meet us at the point, back in Rhodesia and some miles south of Umtali, where the road divides into two branches, one going up into the high veldt, and the other down to Birchenough Bridge and the Sabi.

After the strains of our three days in Salisbury it was ecstasy at last to be on the road, and on our own. The necessity of avoiding Michael and his family, who waylaid us every time we went in or out of the hotel and plied us with perfectly reasonable questions, had made us jumpy. We had developed a strong reluctance for conversation, and a tendency to whisper and glance over our shoulders when speaking to one another in public places. Our shopping had been partially paralysed by a national holiday, which we had not expected, and we had spent a good deal of time in one or other of our bedrooms, receiving our last injections, talking incessantly, and occasionally overcome by hysterical laughter. It was a wonderful relief to be alone at last, packed into the front seat of the Land Rover and driving at speed through a dazzle of sunlit air, a hilly road before us and an empty horizon. Everything, in that sparkling light, seemed new; rolling savannah, distant farms, the dramatic outcrops of granite that broke the plain and breasted the sky like medieval fortresses. Only the dust, for which we had been prepared but which far outdid anything we had imagined, took the fine edge off our pleasure and turned us quickly into mummies of dust with apricot-coloured faces. The Rhodesian roads are made of dust, with two parallel strips of tarmac laid like tramlines, on which one travels. All is well if yours is the only vehicle; the strips are good and the dust lies undisturbed; but as soon as another vehicle comes in sight, both must relinquish the offside tramline in order to pass, and both are enveloped in a dust-storm through which nothing is visible. As all Rhodesians drive extremely fast, and when overtaking in dust cannot possibly see if anything else is coming, there are frequent accidents; and as we had been warned of this, and were going at a speed which everyone else regarded as contemptible, we travelled for many miles in impenetrable fog, enduring the heat with windows closed and coughing plaintively. After a time the traffic dwindled to nothing, and we enjoyed the intoxicating pleasure of running for hours in solitude in the middle of the road, gazing to left and right over the sun-burned landscape as though ours were the only vehicle in creation. How long would the tarmac last? we began to wonder. It came to an end in the moment of framing the question, and we shot on to a plain dust road, ribbed from side to side with deep and mysteriously uniform corrugations. We had been warned about this as well, and advised that the only way to take it was at speed; but our Land Rover was not young, and rattled and shook with such agonizing noises that we could not bear her suffering, and dropped down to a tender twenty miles an hour, tasting each corrugation to the bottom and riding our seats like one of those punitive appliances that had rolled and bucked us in the ship's gymnasium.

We were in no condition when we reached Umtali to present ourselves with decency at the hotel, which was unexpectedly grandiose and disapproving, with too many African servants in red tarbooshes and too many watchful men in tropical suits drinking whisky among too many potted palms on the veranda. Our arrival was not improved by the appearance of our luggage, which had been augmented by a number of ill-packed cardboard boxes, all of which had to be carried up to our rooms (since the Land Rover did not lock) and which shed packets of cornflakes and lavatory paper when handled. We summoned what dignity we could and spent an unprofitable night there, to be shamed all over again by the morning procession of luggage through the palm court. Remembering the dust of the day before we had changed into bush shirts and khaki trousers, and these, deliciously light and cool though they were in the early heat, added another faint discomfort by making us conspicuous, for Umtali is a *de luxe* and urban place, bent on appearing like a tropical Cheltenham, and its women totter about the pavements in high-heeled shoes, more or less looking as though they are going to the races. Still, though we provoked some knowing smiles, 'bush-bashing' is a sport well understood in Umtali, which is the centre of a romantic and mountainous district where sturdy Rhodesians go camping for weeks together; and we were able to repair a few of the omissions which we had already noted with dismay in our equipment. The most serious was that the Land Rover had been sent out without tools of any kind, without even a spanner, and Peter, who had already had difficulty in buying a pick and a crowbar, spent some further exasperated hours alternately fuming and telephoning in a garage. After some argument a full set of tools was promised to follow from Salisbury; for the rest we assumed, when any listed necessity was not to be found, that it was bound to be on the lorry. This comforting belief lost ground as time went on, but we were not yet aware of the full extent of our folly in not personally checking every item.

The road from Umtali to the Portuguese border now ran between hills and rocky heights, through a landscape of considerable splendour; but as soon as the frontier was passed, with its wearisome official delays in the burning sun, it began to drop into lush and cultivated country, steamy and dense and green, with banana plantations and well-tended pineapple fields and roadside paths constantly in motion with groups of walking people. These Africans, so near in distance to the Rhodesian native, yet look quite different, and the change in the appearance of the women is very striking. In Rhodesia women's fashions are a product of the mission school; girls wear a rough approximation to a cotton uniform, and afterwards, in and near the towns, cheap and ugly ready-made cotton dresses, with any piece of utility or finery added—a shrunken cardigan, a blanket or a tablecloth, and, of course, the universal baby-sling, tied tightly across the breasts—flattening and dragging them down and worn incessantly with its sleeping weight from the moment when a little girl is old enough to carry a baby. On the Portuguese side, though the disfiguring method of baby-carrying was universal, an ease and native brilliance was immediately apparent in the dress, which was a cotton kilt swinging below the knees, with odds and ends of different cotton materials wound with considerable gaiety round the body. The Rhodesian women habitually cover their hair with a scarf or scrap of stuff, tightly tied, but the Portuguese women go bare-headed, with close-cropped skulls and many varieties of ear-rings, so that the general effect is freer, more graceful and natural, and infinitely more becoming. Their carriage, like that of African women everywhere, is remarkable for a leisurely, relaxed and stately balance, the naked feet placed softly and steadily in line, the head erect and moving hardly at all, for there is usually something heavy balanced upon it, a water-pot, a bunch of bananas, even a suitcase, while shoulders and arms maintain a sinuous rhythm which cradles the heavy baby on the back. Some of the women sprang off the road as we passed, snatching the bundles and pots off their heads as they did so and waving and laughing at us out of the grass. They seemed delighted with this fleeting glimpse of strangers, and indeed the road from Umtali to Beira must be one of their chief sources of entertainment, running as it does for hundreds of miles without village or turning, a ribbon of communication, across unmarked, ancestral and unchanging bush. They were not the only people who frequented it either, for we would often see, far ahead in the shimmering mirage of some switchback rise, a group of dusky figures squatting in close conference on the road. These, when we approached, would get up with deliberate dignity, and moving off into the grass with measured stride would only at the last reveal themselves as baboons.

We were excited by this first glimpse of the true *indigènes*, and by everything we saw, for there was a holiday feeling about this part of the journey which intoxicated us. We were on our way, with everything still untried, and these first three days were providing a delicious respite. Nothing could possibly worry us at Gorongoza; nobody would question us; nobody could doubt our reason for being there. We had nothing to do but sharpen our unaccustomed senses, and enjoy it.

We had not been going for many hours before I bought, at the cost of an hour's excruciating discomfort, some useful experience. We had stopped to take a drink from our water-bottles and Jack had wandered across the road to admire an unfamiliar and luxuriant creeper which was hanging in bunches of velvet pods from a tree. These unknown beans were extra-ordinarily pretty; as green as moss and covered with delicate velvet. He picked me a spray, and I stroked the pods with my fingers and agreed that they were the prettiest I had seen. A few minutes later my fingers and the palms of my hands began to burn, and I found on examining them that they were covered thickly with almost invisible hairs. I tried to brush these away, but the burning increased, and had now spread to my face, my neck, my forearms and my knees—everywhere, in fact, that my hands in the last few minutes had happened to touch. It was more than burning, it was burning and itching in one, and responded to scratching like a heath-fire to the breeze. In no time at all I was in a desperate state, unable to sit still, trying not to scratch and failing, sighing like a furnace in my restless-ness and indeed feeling horribly like one. I begged Peter to stop, so that I could wring out a cloth in cold water and try for some relief. He obligingly did so, but I could see that he thought I was making a great fuss. His expression of masculine patience deepened perceptibly when I asked again, and by the time I had occasioned a third and then a fourth delay he was sitting with eyes closed and eyebrows raised while I frantically tried every bottle in the medical bag, swabbing myself with cotton-wool and hissing with self-pity. All was of no avail. The damnable itching subsided only with time, dying away without a trace after an hour of misery. We made a resolution that in future we would touch no more unknown plants than we could help, and as we jolted on towards Gorongoza I remembered an ominous remark of Michael's mother—'Everything in Africa has a snag. Bilharzia* in every pool, a crocodile in every river, a thorn in every bush and snakes everywhere.' I could have wished she had thought to mention the buffalo bean, which I had so innocently fondled, and which we all of us came to know more intimately later.

Gorongoza embraces two thousand square miles of varied country, forest, plain and swamp, all of it flat. It has no fence or boundary and the animals wander out or in at will, but show little inclination to stray, for inside the reserve they are wholly unmolested and food is plentiful. It is run with efficiency by the Portuguese Government, is expensive to stay at, and heavily booked for the whole of the dry season. Chitengo, the rest camp, accommodates about fifty visitors at a time, in 'rondavels' which are sophisticated adaptations of native huts, and in concrete bungalows with shower-baths. The camp is surrounded by barbed-wire fencing and is closed at sundown: there has been no accident so far, and the Portuguese, their eyes on the tourist revenue, do not wish for any. For the rest, there is a fancy bar with an outside terrace which does its best, with coloured tables and sunshades, to look like a resort, and a restaurant in which one eats wholesome and uninteresting meals. There is also an office, presided over by a handsome young

---

* Bilharzia is a microscopic parasite which spends one phase of its career under the shell of the tiny water-snails infesting African rivers, especially in places where the flow is sluggish. If it invades the human body, by being drunk in unboiled water or by getting in under the nails or through a scratch in the skin, it causes a long-drawn wasting disease and finally death. No precaution is effective against it except thoroughly boiling all drinking and washing water, and not going into the rivers. It causes widespread ill-health and early death among Africans, and is difficult to treat because the symptoms often appear for the first time several years after infection, by which time it is too late.

Portuguese in well-pressed shorts and hand-sewn moccasins, and an African clerk who does a brisk trade in 'native' souvenirs of a mass-produced and cynical description.

We three were allotted one of the bungalows, of two bedrooms with a washroom and shower-bath in between. The bedrooms were furnished with the most striking economy we had seen anywhere, each containing two beds, a small bedside table and mat, and nothing else. One sat and slept on the bed, and kept one's clothes and possessions on the bed or on the floor, a choice which presented a certain difficulty, for it was too hot to bear anything on the bed beside oneself, and the floor was not conspicuously clean. Neither, however, by this time, were we; so it did not greatly matter.

The routine of life in the reserve is simple and regular; there are two trips a day with a native guide, with an interval for food and sleep in the afternoon. It is wise to leave the camp at first light, for this is the time when diurnal creatures first come out to feed, and the lions, who have been out all night, are coming home. The animals keep fairly strictly to their areas— zebra and wildbeeste on the open plain, where speed and distance are their safety, lions in the jungle grass at the plain's edge, where they can lie unseen, elephants in the forest where vegetation is thick and the light poor and they are almost invisible. The advantage of taking a guide, which you are not obliged to do, is that he not only knows the maze of vehicle tracks in which it is easy to be lost, but knows also where the game is likely to be, and has a highly trained faculty for seeing, hearing and smelling it. One goes everywhere by car, and is not supposed to get out, though it is safe enough in areas where there are neither lions nor elephants.

The lion is the great spoiled *blasé* star of Gorongoza, following a way of life which suits him to perfection and tolerating sight-seers because they are really a very minor inconvenience. The teeming herds of zebra are all his, the hartebeeste, the waterbuck, the impala. Man does not compete with him as a hunter, but

comes and goes respectfully in a motor-car, a harmless phenomenon of which he takes no notice. At Gorongoza he is still,
or has the illusion of being, a king. The lions have even taken
over the old rest camp, abandoned when the present one was
built, and several prides inhabit the empty cottages. They lie
flattened on the cement floors in the heat of the day, gazing out
through the broken doorways with an expression of languor;
sometimes upside down with limp paws in the air, steadily
regarding the intruder out of the tops of their eyes. They have
everything there that a zoo can offer except bars, and not a
cottage is vacant. The principal bungalow has an outside stair-
case and a flat roof, and as soon as the evening air is cool enough
the pair of lionesses who inhabit the parlour go nimbly upstairs
and sit on the roof, yawning from a heavy meal and a too-long
siesta, tasting the first faint breeze and deducing from it, perhaps,
the movements of the zebra. The herds of zebra are so large
that the lion is assured a lifetime of good living. He has only to
kill and eat them, and no one could doubt the success of his
hunting who has seen family after family sleeping off the effects
of the night's kill. The lions we saw in the early morning were
all prone and bulging; it was difficult, if one wanted to take
photographs, to find one on its feet. They would lift a massive
head out of the yellow grass if the Land Rover crept imper-
tinently close, and as often as not would let it fall back again, as
though drunk. Cubs were shyer than adults, and would quickly
become uneasy and slink away, and this in turn would suggest to
their sleep-sodden mothers that they ought to get up and follow,
which they usually did, with a look of justifiable annoyance;
but the male lions, once they had taken the weight off their feet,
were impervious to sightseers, and showed impatience only if
one were ill-mannered enough to talk or make a noise with a
camera.

On our second morning, when we had gone out before six
o'clock and the sun had just risen, we saw a pride of lions coming
home from the kill and stopping to drink at a pool on the open

plain. We were sitting in the Land Rover, watching a distant
herd of zebra through field-glasses, when five shadows, very
close to the ground, came into the field of vision and went down
to the pool. It was a big lion, two young and handsome lionesses
and two half-grown cubs. Though cautious, and making themselves rather flat like stalking cats, the females and cubs took
little notice of us. These lions have never seen a gun, and do not
associate motor-cars with man. The male lion ignored us completely, striding deliberately past when he had drunk all he
wanted and throwing himself down conspicuously in the shade
of some palms. The sky was already busy with wheeling
vultures, and some nervy and elegant jackals were trotting in
long sweeps round the inner conclave of hunched forms who
were finishing off the zebra with much ill-tempered spreading of
wings, abusive squawks and ungainly predatory jumps at one
another. When we passed by on our way back to camp there was
nothing left but some ribbons of satin-striped skin and a delicate
skeleton.

On the last night before we left Salisbury we had dined with
Michael's parents and an agreeable young man, son of an old
friend, who was learning his Africa from the privileged view-
point of aide-de-camp to a Governor. It being established that
we were going on safari, and for the first time, the talk had
naturally turned on the hairbreadth escapes from death which
the three of them had (it seemed, repeatedly) suffered, it being a
natural human instinct to wish to alarm the beginner as much as
possible. They had all been mauled by either leopard or lion,
or had at least assisted at a mauling; deadly snakes had dropped
on them from trees; their dogs had been devoured by crocodiles;
their bearers had fled when they were cornered by wild pig, and
they had been charged almost monotonously by elephant,
buffalo and rhino. We remembered all their stories now that we
were wandering in a reserve more thickly populated with wild
game than any area open to hunting safaris; but in spite of the
great herds that we watched from under the palms and fever-

trees, in spite of the smell of lion in the long grass and the neat round fibrous packages of elephant dung, twice as big as a cocoanut, that from time to time we found moist and fresh in our path, it was almost impossible to feel the stimulus of danger. African boys whose work is to clear the paths go far afield in the forest and sleep under shelters of branches and palm fronds. 'There is no danger for them,' said the young Portuguese in the office, 'unless an elephant treads on them in the dark. That, of course, can happen.' The lions are too preoccupied to be dangerous (though it is unwise to get out of one's car); the rhinos are few and so unreasonably nervous that they have been seen, even by the Game Warden, only twice in a number of years; and the elephants, which are numerous, are peaceable on the whole and confine themselves to those parts of the forest where they are not easily seen. However, they can be irritable, and are more sensitive about their privacy than lions. We had been told that they dislike the sound of a running engine, but our guide, who spoke a few words of English, told us that we must not stall or turn off our engine when we were near elephants, since it was sometimes important to get away very quickly.

We drove gingerly every afternoon through those parts of the forest which elephants were known to frequent, the three of us in front and Francisco, our guide, peering and occasionally pointing over our shoulders. We tried to ask him what we should do if, at a turning in the path, we should meet an elephant coming from the other direction; but his English was unequal to this, and my Portuguese phrase book offered nothing which had any bearing on this question. We met no elephants on the paths, though their bale-like droppings punctuated our progress and showed that at least they used the paths at night: in the day they preferred to browse their way steadily through the intricate undergrowth; and it was here, rising like islands out of a sea of green, that we eventually found them, a herd of five, moving majestically through a screen of trees and leaving a trail of torn branches behind them. We stopped the Land Rover, keeping the engine running, and saw the elephants pause in their progress and lift up their trunks like croziers in our direction, delicately sifting the air. Unalarmed, they twined their trunks back into the branches and went on, and we edged ourselves quietly forward a yard at a time, keeping them well in sight. We could see them clearly now, a tall elephant with a calf moving at her heels, another of equal size, and several apparently half-grown ones behind. As they moved out of our range of vision, so we followed them, Francisco urging us gently forward with movements of his hand and Peter determined to leave the wheel and get out for just a moment with his box Brownie. We were now well into the trees, when the leading elephant suddenly got tired of us. She turned, flapping her ears and throwing her trunk dramatically into the air, making at the same time a hateful noise like badly changing gears. For a split second I thought that something hellish had gone wrong with the car, until I found that the noise was the elephant trumpeting, and that she was advancing heavily towards us through the bushes. 'Keep going, boss, keep going,' said Francisco urgently, but the only way, unless we were to charge the elephant, was to go backwards, and this we did, in a series of eccentric leaps, mangling branches, glancing off trees, Peter straining to see out of the back window, Francisco shouting 'Keep going!' and all of us too suddenly thrown together to have much idea of the whereabouts of the elephant. Fortunately elephants are usually satisfied with a short display of temper (though we did not remember this at the time and discovered afterwards that we had all, in a moment of panic, been visited in a flash by one of the Salisbury stories, which ended with the words, 'stamped the car flat into the ground, like an old tin can') and the massive creature, seeing us in full and horrified retreat, soon tired of the demonstration and went back with a justified air to her quiet browsing.

We sorted ourselves out as soon as this was feasible, all talking at once and laughing a little too shrilly, like people who by their own fault have just missed being run over, and found Francisco as ludicrously breathless as the rest of us. 'They are dangerous,' he said at last, laughing and wiping his eyes, and this really seemed to sum up the impressions of all of us. We had been lucky to get so easily out of a tight corner, and our feelings of awe were increased when Peter pointed out that we had been charged by elephant. We considered this unexpected aspect, and were impressed.

'Are you really sure that that would count as a charge?'

'Certainly. What else do you suppose the brute was doing?'

'I imagined a charge as being more determined, somehow. Involving trampling.'

'You will have to be satisfied with this. It could have trampled if it had wanted.'

'So you really think we can say we have been charged by elephant? Like everybody at dinner?'

'Of course we can. I mean we have. And if you hear me saying so, I'll thank you not to throw any doubts on the story.'

In a sense this little episode gave us the feeling that we had earned a sort of passport that we needed. The visit to Gorongoza had been a feint, though an enjoyable one, and now, as well as establishing that we had gone into Portuguese territory for a conventional purpose, it had furnished us besides with several little histories of our own, which we sensed would be useful when we rejoined Michael. So far, in Africa, we had had very little to talk about besides the things that could be spoken of only alone, and now we felt we were equipped with conversation, which could be spun into a firm fabric of protection.

We needed it after leaving Gorogonza, for our last precautionary operation before joining Michael was to make a short stay near Penhalonga in the hope (or perhaps the fear) of learning what had happened to Bob Bullock. We knew from Russell's narrative that his principal partner, Ned Bullock, was dead; but Bob Bullock, the brother, had married and settled down before the First World War, and though it was unlikely that he was still alive he might have left a family, who in turn might know something about the old adventure, or who might even have (it was possible) Russell's diary. We had taken the precaution, in Salisbury, of going through the appropriate section of the telephone directory, and were relieved, I think, rather than otherwise to find that there was no such subscriber in Penhalonga. I think we rather hoped that we should find nothing, for if Bob Bullock were still alive or his children there, Russell's name would have been difficult to mention. They might guess at once what had brought us to Africa, or, worse still, tell us that the treasure was no longer there and had been long ago discovered. Or they might only exchange significant glances, and say nothing. We built up a morbid picture of them as secretive and rich, uneasy when the name of Russell was mentioned and not at all pleased to see us. Would we be able to ask about the diary after all this time, on the specious grounds that Russell was my uncle? I would have had to attempt it, of course, if we had come on its tracks; such a detailed check on the later narrative would have been invaluable; but I was thankful when we drew a blank in the telephone directory. Still, we knew that we must inquire more thoroughly than that, and planned to spend two nights in the near neighbourhood of Penhalonga, staying with someone to whom Peter had a rather roundabout introduction. This lady was a tobacco-farmer, an English widow who managed her own estate; and when we learned that she also made room for a few paying guests we proposed ourselves for a visit after Gorogonza, asking her also to find out for us if there were any people called Bullock living in the neighbourhood.

It was with some anxiety that we took the long hot dusty road back into Rhodesia, for our carefree diversion was now over and everything from now on would be part of a progress towards an incalculable end. We were thirsty, dusty and tired long before we had reached the road for Penhalonga, and had not improved our condition by drinking cold beer in a dirty bar *en route* and recklessly eating the fierily peppered shrimps which the Portuguese proprietor had pressed upon us. We looked, and felt, unpresentable, and became conscious of this when our dusty vehicle ran into the courtyard of a long low farmhouse with a pillared portico where elderly ladies and dogs were sitting in the shade. One saw right through the house to a brilliant garden with a view of fields and hills and romantic highlands, and before we had had time to taste the full contrast between ourselves and this we had been shepherded into familiar country-house bedrooms, all chintz and jugs of flowers and little pictures, and were refreshing ourselves with a trolley of tea in private—lace-edged cloth, walnut cake, excellent dropscones and butter and blackcurrant jam. It was like one of those trick pictures that used to appear long ago in children's annuals: one way up we were in Africa, every nerve of our bodies alive to the surrounding strangeness; the other way up we were having tea in Gloucestershire.

All this in itself was a sort of bizarre pleasure, which we were able to enjoy once it was established that our hostess had not been able to hear of any Bullocks in the neighbourhood—'except some people who used to be here, I believe, but they went away years ago.' She knew nothing of them, and accepted the inquiry as springing from natural interest in some long-ago wartime acquaintance of Peter's father. We turned with relief to our Gorogonza episodes, which proved to be splendid fuel for conversation. There was a retired tobacco-planter staying among the several ladies in the house, a seasoned sportsman and expert on all the sights we ought to see in Africa; he responded to fresh blood as though our presence had given him a magical transfusion. He put us through a course of questions, too eager to advise to be able to wait for the answers. The direction we thought of taking was not the smallest use. We must go somewhere else. We must go to Victoria Falls. We must see Rhodes's tomb. We must follow the Garden Route. Mozambique was a dead loss, we mustn't think of it. Zimbabwe, which I had cautiously mentioned, was 'a bore—just like an old brickworks.' He droned happily on, fountaining advice. How many servants were we taking? Were they any good? He was disappointed to learn there were only three. 'Some of them are all right,' he said, 'but one has to know how to handle them. One must remember these Africans have only just dropped from the trees.' On the second evening a dread of his questions and advice began to oppress me, but Gorongoza came once more to our rescue, and we were soon listening in silence to sagas of lion and crocodile, of elephant and buffalo and pig, to our relief and the sportsman's satisfaction.

4

Russell's Country

WE had arranged to meet Michael at a road junction some forty or fifty miles south of Umtali, and here indeed we found him—rather to our surprise, for we had received several garbled and mysterious telephone messages to the effect that he was delayed, or the cook was delayed, or that there was something wrong with the lorry. The lorry was impressive, looking as though it were on its way to relieve a garrison, piled to a great height with boxes and gear and things which lurched and bulged under a green tarpaulin. In the crevices of this travelling store-room, in the utmost discomfort but glad at least to be out of the blazing sun, were our three Africans, clutching little cardboard suitcases and fending off the wooden boxes which incessantly and painfully fell down on them. Michael was driving, looking more splendid than ever now that we saw him in the open, with his cartridge-belt and boots and leather leggings, his broad-brimmed hat tilted rakishly over the eyes and a scarlet hand-kerchief negligently knotted at the throat. Beside him in the cab, occupying the passenger seat with an air of authority, was a large Alsatian dog whose name was Shadow and who also, we learned, was a member of the police. That is to say, he belonged to

Michael and went with him almost everywhere. Never was a dog, it seemed, more dedicated to his profession. If he were not a full and official member of the British South African Police, he did not know it.

We set off now in convoy, but with a sufficient distance between the vehicles to keep the Land Rover out of range of the lorry's dust. We were heading for the hill country, the high veldt through which Russell had travelled when leaving Portuguese territory. These were the foothills which, farther east, ran up to about six thousand feet and became the Chimanimani Mountains; the invisible frontier ran diagonally through them. Mount Selinda, the missionary station which Russell had mentioned in his narrative, was in the midst of these, at the three thousand level, in a tract of tropical rain forest. We had thought a great deal about Mount Selinda and its missionaries. All that we knew of them was that they were Americans and Protestant; we did not suppose that they would help us if they knew what we were looking for; on the contrary, it was more probable that they would put unthought-of ethical difficulties in our way; but we did imagine that they would have a sound working knowledge of the country and might indirectly be able to help us a great deal. It would be foolish to neglect any local information that might be picked up at the station. Since leaving Salisbury, however, Peter had spent some time brooding over the War Office map of the area, and had come to the conclusion, from his general feeling for the direction in which Umgila's country probably lay, that we would do better to address ourselves to another mission, Chikore, which we could see at a point perhaps fifteen miles south-west of Mount Selinda, in the unforested foothills to the east of the Sabi. Russell had never mentioned Chikore, and this seemed strange, for it was nearer than Mount Selinda to the area which we privately thought of as his country; but we had already learned that Peter had an eye for terrain, and that his brain received messages from even the most inadequate map which ours did not; so we bowed to his instinctive feeling that Chikore and not Mount Selinda was the place to make for. As it turned out he was perfectly right, and the reason that Russell had never mentioned it was probably, as we learned later, that it was a very much smaller and younger mission than the other, and may even not have been there at the time of Russell's journey through the territory.

The country through which we followed the lorry changed its character dramatically every few miles, as though bent on showing us every bizarre variety. At first the road, a passably good one, ran like a new-made gash through a forest of scrub, endlessly up and down over switchback hills, with a perilously narrow cement bridge over a dried-up rocky stream-bed in each of the bottoms. Then for an hour or so the soil was a uniform light grey, smooth and hard, as though it were made of asbestos, pricked out with a few parched bushes and scattered with stones; then it was suddenly bright red clay, ridged and veined with erosion, piling up in steep banks on either side of the road, overhung with lush and extravagant vegetation. Native huts here, when one caught a glimpse of thatch among the green, were set about with banana and papaya, the huge leaves bright as banners in the heat. Then without warning of change, it was open country again, with splendid rocky kopjes on either side, some thickly forested and some clothed in scrub, and all of them crowned with rosy heights and crags.

Michael had been down here before, while we were at Penhalonga, and had already chosen the site for our first camp. This was on a bank of the Tanganda River, and to reach it we left the road, bumped through a dusty native kraal which seemed to have no one in it but chickens and children, crossed a harvested mealie-patch still bearing the tattered remnants of stalks and foliage, and came to rest on a level grassy bank, set about with bare and monstrous baobab trees. A person who has never come face to face with a baobab can have no idea of the strangeness of the spectacle. They are grey in colour, of immense girth, and so gross in shape as to be rather shocking. The higher they grow the bigger they seem to get, in grotesque defiance of the usual habit of trees, and their bare swollen branches (for this season of dry heat was their winter, and they were leafless) writhe off from the summit in all directions, looking for all the world like upturned roots. There is an African legend to explain the baobab, which certainly looks as though it needed explaining. God was so angry with the sins of the people that he took all the trees away as a punishment, so that they should have no shade. He was softened eventually by their prayers and repentance and agreed to put the trees back, but in doing so, as a warning and a reminder, planted all the baobabs upside-down. Seen naked, with the root-like branches gnarling against the sky, one would say that that is exactly what has happened. I delighted in their appearance but never became entirely reconciled to their strangeness, which has a sinister quality, like the threatening trees in a *Red Riding Hood* pantomime: it would not be out of character if a baobab were to lower a distorted arm and claw up a victim.

Though surrounded by these leafless monsters the place was fresh with shade, for there were several fine specimens of a noble-looking tree as well, about the size and shape of an English chestnut, covered with dark foliage and vermilion flowers not unlike rhododendrons, with heavy pods the size of rolling-pins hung freakishly here and there; and it was in the shade of these that our tents were commodiously set. There were two tents, a good distance apart, each under its particular tree; Peter and Michael were to occupy one and Jack and I the other. Our three boys, it appeared, would sleep in the lorry, where they had some odds and ends of bundles and blankets which did not look at all comfortable, but which Michael assured us they preferred to the bother of erecting a third tent. Ours already had a pair of camp beds inside, made up with blankets and sheets in the proper fashion, and the cook had set out a metal-topped table with a cloth and four canvas chairs, so that it all began to look luxurious and safari-like. The cook himself, too, was very magnificent, disguised from head to foot in a chef's white outfit, in which he moved with slow dignity through the long grass, bringing tea on a tin tray with an organdie tray-cloth, and a plate of biscuits artistically arranged. He did everything slowly and with an air of melancholy, watched in every movement by a group of baboons on a sandy cliff on the other side of the river, sitting close together in a row, as though at the circus. It seemed rather ridiculous in these surroundings to be sitting round a plastic table-cloth drinking tea; but there was no doubt, from the gravity of his deportment, that the cook felt that the correct thing was being done, that we were behaving as people did who went on safari, and that his dignity was sustained by the repeated slow traverses that he made, bringing a little hot water or an extra teaspoon.

Presently the sun set, and there was a moment of delusive dusk, and then it was dark. Shorty had dug a trench and built a fire in it, and his muscular figure, with shirt-tails hanging out of his shorts at the back, was seen in silhouette against the blaze, dragging up lengths of tree-trunk and rolling and kicking them into the right position. A cloud of bats came out of the trees and flickered and swooped about in the light of the fire, flying high up, on the edge of the rosy smoke. The river kept up a continuous murmur and the baboons barked with surprise from time to time; we could no longer see them in the surrounding dark but we could tell that they were there. Presently the cook brought across a fine bright gas-lamp from his kitchen quarters, and its brilliant moon, phosphorescent and greenish, isolated us still more from the surrounding darkness. I had the feeling that we were being watched by more than baboons, and no doubt we were, for occasionally we would hear a murmur or a smothered laugh, and a twig would crack which had not been cracked by the fire.

Michael, who was too young and too energetic to sit still for long, and who had been stumbling about in the darkness ever since he had finished his tea, now reappeared in the circle of lamp-light, his thumbs in his cartridge-belt, and announced that he had been bargaining for a goat. It was, he said, a good idea to have fresh meat whenever the opportunity offered, and to save our stores. He had bought a nice little goat for fifteen shillings, and we would have part of it for supper. Even before he had finished speaking the goat, which was indeed small and very young, was led bleating into the camp, where it was received with delighted laughter by our three boys, who began arguing excitedly and lugging it about with vigour in the shadows. I retired into my tent and lit a candle. I did not know how they would kill the goat, but I imagined they would cut its throat and I did not wish to be present. It had a very childish voice and its cries were unnerving. I put my trust in Michael, whom I could see from where I sat on the edge of the bed, standing hugely in the firelight, hands on hips, watching whatever it was that the boys were doing. It would soon be over, I thought; but the laughter and the bleating dreadfully continued, and presently Michael came over, a little abashed, and asked whether any of us knew any method of killing a goat. The boys, it seemed, had never done it before, and although they were willing to try were already so far gone in giggles that he doubted whether they would make a job of it. He himself, he said, had never killed anything at close quarters like that, and he didn't fancy blowing it to pieces with his rifle. So in the end it was Peter with one of our revolvers who put an end to the goat's anguish, and it was slung up at once to the branch of a tree in the beam of the Land Rover's searchlight and skinned in a dancing cloud of flying insects.

Early next morning, in the brief half-light before sunrise, the deputy headman of the village presented himself as guide and took Jack off into the hills to shoot guinea-fowl. He proved to be a charming and courteous character, in freshly washed green shirt and khaki shorts, and, like every African villager that we met, he was frankly delighted to see that we had rifles. Firearms are forbidden to the ordinary African, only a chief being allowed to possess a shot-gun, and even chiefs are kept deliberately short of ammunition. This means that the small wild game that Africans long for must either be trapped or shot with a bow and arrow, and consequently meat is the greatest of all luxuries. A stranger with a shot-gun or a rifle is a man to cherish, for it is etiquette that he should ask permission to shoot, should accept a guide, and share whatever he kills with the headman of the village. His camping near-by may mean that by evening there will be fresh meat for everyone.

In this area, however, game is scarce, as we had been warned it would be. The Government had cleared it of tsetse-fly only by taking the drastic course of shooting or driving out all the wild game and temporarily forbidding the keeping of domestic cattle. This had robbed the lion and the leopard of their living; they had followed the wild buck over the border into Portuguese territory, where there was no tsetse-fly control and predators could do pretty much as they liked. They were only just, said the headman, beginning to come back. There were buck now in the hills above the river, and the leopards were helping themselves to goats in the night. He hoped very much for meat from one of our guns, but the only game which Jack saw in the course of two long early morning forays was eland; a noble bull and two cows pacing majestically along the brow of a hill, upwind of the hunters and so unconscious of them. Jack had no intention of killing anything like this, and watched them go with pleasure, admiring their beauty. The headman was disappointed, but too polite to say more than that it was a pity. He led him a long way above the valley to a place he knew as a favourite roost of guinea-fowl; they exploded out of the grass and trees as he predicted, heavy as pheasants but clumsier, flying stupidly after the long and chilly night. They were shot with ease and brought back to the camp in limp handfuls, warm bunches of grey and miraculously spotted plumage, and the headman carried his share back to the village.

By seven o'clock we were sitting down to breakfast under the trees, glad to be out of our tents, which caught the early sun and were like ovens. It was an interminable meal: the cook wished us to begin with cornflakes and tinned peaches, then to proceed to goat's liver, bacon and fried tomatoes, which were certainly delicious but took an unconscionable time to produce. Each article—bread, butter, weak tea, salt, marmalade—was brought separately on a tray, the cook dressed as before and stepping with slow care through the long grass between his kitchen and our table, which were a considerable distance apart. We were hungry and ate everything, Michael yelling from time to time, boss-fashion, for more butter, more hot water or more milk, and the cook answering the summons with deliberation, staring morosely at Michael, whose ringing voice and lordly ways he appeared to resent. By the time we had finished it was nine o'clock and our shirts were patched with sweat. If meals were to be conducted at this pace and in this manner, it seemed that the days would have to be given up to consuming them, and that nothing else would be possible. Already the cook was gravely bargaining with a beautiful young woman who had appeared shyly behind a tree with a couple of fowls, and was now kneeling respectfully at his feet, her baby on her back, offering the birds in both hands and answering him in a soft voice and with the most ravishing of smiles. I never saw another such beauty in all the time we were in Africa, so slender-necked, so patrician in feature, with such enormous eyes; and it crossed my mind that perhaps she was more Zulu than Mashona, and that Umgila's warriors might have been her ancestors. It was tempting to imagine the Countess looking like this, and perhaps the cook was not wholly unmoved by her appearance, for after prolonged discussion he bought the fowls, which when dinner came proved to have been very old ones.

We were by this time anxious to move on, for however pleasant our camp, with running water and shade, it was no-where near the area where we wanted to be, and the three of us were secretly getting restless. Breaking camp so soon, however, was out of the question, and Michael seemed surprised that we should want it. The *munts* had by now totally unpacked the lorry and strewn everything in inconceivable confusion in the grass. Nothing seemed to have been packed with any system; everything was mixed together in a score of tea-chests, so that when anything was wanted they had emptied half a dozen boxes before they found it, and the stuff was thrown back higgledy-piggledy, without the least attempt at method or order. In the midst of this rich wreckage the cook kept his state, with a large meat-safe full of bananas (I never discovered why he found it necessary to keep bananas in the meat-safe; the meat was invariably hung from the branch of a tree), a small refrigerator which ran on paraffin, a Calor gas-stove and a few rather thin and inadequate-looking saucepans. There was also a large dog-kennel, which was supposed to be for Shadow, but which the cook used for keeping sacks of sugar in, and any dead guinea-fowl or live chickens which were waiting for the pot. Sacks of potatoes, bags of flour and mealie-meal lay round him as he worked, and were kicked, sat on or walked over as occasion demanded. He had a fire continuously burning in a trench, but scorned to cook on this; it was used for boiling kettles and heating washing water. One had to agree, after taking a quick look at these essential arrangements, that packing up would be a long day's work, and that to move after only one night's camp was unreasonable. It was not wholly easy, either, to convince Michael, for, seen simply from the point of view of safari, the site was good, and he knew better than we did that in the dry season this was sufficiently rare. Besides, he was excited by the eland that Jack had seen, and was sure that we should find duiker buck in the hills. We would eat well there, he said, and he would even show us the proper way of making biltong. Rhodesians have an almost mystical reverence for biltong, which they carry in the pocket and chew like tobacco, but even this enticement was abandoned at last, and it was agreed that we should leave for Chikore the next morning.

There was a town, Chipinga, to be passed on the way; the

last we should see, for all beyond was bush. We approached it with some misgiving, for in one of the official pamphlets we had studied in London it had been fulsomely described, and in such a way as to make us fear that this outpost might be the death of all our hopes. It was the centre, said the pamphlet, of a vast development scheme, a sort of settlers' paradise spreading its civilizing influence across the hills. Schools, hospitals, hotels, modern housing, new roads and residential areas were mentioned, and the crowning glory, which made us even more uneasy, was a nine-hole golf-course. If such an urban development had taken place, within forty or fifty miles of Umgila's village, what hope had we of finding the old sites, which perhaps now lay beneath metalled roads and petrol stations? What hope would we have of pursuing our search unseen, on the cement pavements of a settler's suburbia, between the all-night café and the cinema? We need not have worried. Chipinga, like Martin Chuzzlewit's Eden, was not all built, and fell quite touchingly short of its Utopian description. It was, in fact, a short, straight, wide and dusty street, bordered by a few one-storey buildings of impermanent appearance and by two garages, one on either side, littered with the rusting skeletons of cars. The only live and prosperous-looking things about the town were its motor-cars, which were mostly large, shining and American, the property of farmers who had come in to collect their mail, pick up a spare part, do a little shopping at Meikles' store or go to the bank. If, instead of these, there had been a few dejected-looking horses hitched to posts, the main street might have served as a set for an early silent Western; and there were moments, as we improved acquaintance with the place, when we felt that to shoot it out with the inhabitants from the top of the Land Rover was the only means of breaking its stifling calm. Instead, on this first occasion, we went innocently into Meikles' store to buy cartridges, and our own calm was shattered soon enough.

We had left Salisbury in the happy belief, fostered by Michael's father, that as we intended to shoot only small game for the pot, no permits were needed. To shoot an elephant, or a rhino, or a crocodile, or indeed anything that people on hunting safaris wish to shoot (with one exception, the lion, which is classed as vermin) one must first buy a permit, varying in price according to the kind of animal one hopes to kill. A twenty-five-pound permit entitles one to buffalo or zèbra or the like, fifty pounds covers 'royal game'—elephant, rhino, leopard, eland, waterbuck, crocodile and so on, the numbers being determined by the Game Department locally according to the supply of game in a given area, and taking into consideration the value of the animal. In 'native districts', those usually not conspicuously fertile areas of Rhodesia which are given over solely to African farming and habitation, the shooting of game is generally prohibited, and hunting safaris give them a wide berth. Part of the disgust with our expedition which Michael's father had so civilly tried to conceal had been due to the fact that we had disclaimed any desire to shoot big game, royal or otherwise, and were moreover planning to spend most of our time in native territory. Obviously, he said, we would not need permits; nobody was going to waste time worrying about the kind of small vermin we were likely to shoot. Nevertheless, when we took stock of our ammunition at Chipinga, having expended only a few rounds on the Tanganda guinea-fowl, we were surprised to find that there was very little left, and that the heavy boxes on which we were comfortably depending contained shot of formidable size (suitable perhaps for ostrich?) and enormous rifle bullets, both hard and soft-nosed, of the sort that are recommended for elephant and rhino. This was the sort of thing that was always happening to us. To expect to find any given part of our equipment simply because it was down on the typewritten list, soon became for us one of those superstitions which nobody in his right mind subscribes to, and we never unpacked a box or delved into a tea-chest without the most cynical misgivings; but the almost complete absence of the kind of shot we had specified

C

was a disagreeable surprise, and we were thankful that we had found out the discrepancy while we were still at Chipinga. Accordingly we applied to the general store for reinforcements, and were taken aback when we were refused further cartridges without permission from the Commissioner for Native Affairs.

This important personage turned out to be a small dark unsmiling unfriendly official, dressed like a town clerk and housed in a bare bungalow in the police compound. One look at his stony expression, which deepened in displeasure as we introduced ourselves, was enough to bring rushing to our minds the ominous words at the end of Russell's narrative—'Beware especially of Native Commissioners and their spies.' We had never meant to go near one, or foreseen the necessity to do so, and here we were standing helplessly in the creature's office, and he was not at all pleased to see us. He asked at once for the registration numbers of our vehicles and when he had carefully written these down, asked us coldly why we had not informed him of our presence in his area. He studied the point of his pencil while we explained that we were making a purely private journey and had not known that this was necessary, and then wrote for some minutes under cover of his blotting-paper. It was essential, he said at last, that he should know where every car was in his area; and why. We should have reported to him on arriving at Chipinga, and must keep him informed of our movements so long as we remained in the district. We had no business whatever to have shot anything, not even guinea-fowl, and we must certainly, he said, looking hard at Michael, have been aware of this. We explained, with many civil apologies, that we had really not understood this, and that all we had shot was a few birds for the pot. We were now asking for his permission to buy a little more ammunition for the same purpose, as we were going to be a long time out in the bush and might sometimes need to supplement our rations. He looked for a long time at Michael's cartridge-belt before replying, and something like a suggestion of pleasure came into his face. Permission was refused. He sprang to his feet and went to the map on the wall. Here, he said, pointing to two remote areas a long way to the north, he was prepared to allow us to shoot an occasional bird, nothing more. The fact that we were not going to be anywhere near these areas seemed to gratify him. Where *were* we going, then? We said we were undecided. He came back to the table to make a note of this, and the interview was over.

We trailed back up the dusty street with mixed feelings. It was an abominable piece of luck that the mistakes made in Salisbury over our ammunition should have landed us in the arms of the one man in the region whom we most wanted to avoid. He had not liked the look of us, that was evident; and was annoyed that he had not been officially consulted. Now he would believe that, having failed to obtain permission to shoot for food, we would be tempted to do a little discreet poaching, and we had an uneasy feeling that the 'spies' whom Russell had mentioned (whoever they might be) were probably already receiving their instructions.

However, there was nothing to be done about it, except perhaps to leave Chipinga as quickly as possible, before he should have time for further obstructive thoughts. This we did, pausing only to do a little unofficial ammunition deal with a Greek storekeeper in a back street, and to fortify ourselves with lunch in Chipinga's solitary hotel. Unpromising though it looked, this one-storey dump proved unexpectedly sympathetic, for it was clean and not uncomfortable, and the catering was tackled by the Italian proprietor and his wife in a spirited attempt to provide something resembling Italian food and at the same time satisfy the Rhodesian appetite. The two do not, of course, go together, but the good people were trying; and our first experience of a meal in this frontier town gave us an insight into the magnitude of the problem. The luncheon menu, which offered no alternatives and was an arbitrary succession of courses, was as follows:

AVOCADO PEAR
TOMATO SOUP
BAKED FISH IN TOMATO
KIDNEYS ON TOAST
CURRIED MEAT AND RICE
PORK CHOPS, VEGETABLES AND SALAD
CHOCOLATE PUDDING
CHEESE AND BISCUITS
POT OF TEA

We tried to refuse a number of the courses, but this caused disastrous confusion among the African waiters, who thought that we were finding fault with the food, and appealed to the proprietor. If one of us did succeed in rejecting a dish, we were not brought the next course, which we had asked for, but were kept waiting until it fell due in its proper time. One of us could not, for instance, choose curry and cancel the chops, while the other decided on pork chops and did not want curry. If we insisted, the inexorable order of the menu was still maintained, the pork-chop customer having to sit and wait while the other ate his way through a mound of curry, and the curry-fancier having to take his turn at waiting while the other fought his way through two pork chops of enormous size, three vegetables, and a salad. This is not a happy social arrangement, but we could see that it was our fault; all round us in the dining-room dusty-haired men in shorts with weathered faces were eating steadily through the luncheon from beginning to end without argument or fuss and drinking tall bottles of beer into the bargain. We wondered how such lavish catering could pay, for this meal was by no means expensive. Fortunately the proprietor did not notice our puny behaviour, and embraced the chance of conversation when we went out to settle the bill. He and his wife had come from Como about fifteen years ago; the country, he said, was fine, but business was poor; there were 'no plenty people'. His solution was for the government to allow lots and lots of industrious Italians in, though he admitted that jobs for Europeans were hard to get, since people could employ Africans for less money. He was immensely proud of being a naturalized Rhodesian. 'My child no speaka English like I do. They speaka like you. They Rhodesians, justa like you.' We felt obscurely proud of this ourselves, the more so as we were momentarily on our own, without Michael, who was paying a social call at the police barracks; but on second thoughts credit was more probably due to our authentic-looking khaki shirts and dusty Land Rover. He took it for granted, like the District Commissioner, that we were on a hunting expedition, and saw us off with cheery admonishments to 'shoota plenty lion'.

As soon as we left Chipinga the road began to climb, drawing itself steadily upwards into thick woods where the soil was red and moist. The air became cooler; one could taste that it was no longer sterile with heat, but had the memory of last night's dew on it, the promise of dews to come. After about three hours we passed a number of native stores at the roadside, cubes of white-washed brick about the size of cowsheds, just big enough to hold a counter and open shelves, and judged that we must be approaching Chikore Mission. Other evidences soon appeared; groups of girls in cotton gym-tunics stirring up the dust of the road with bare feet; young men on bicycles who dismounted as we approached and raised a disciplined hand; scores of native huts in groups by the roadside and a general purposeful movement of coming and going. We slowed the vehicles down by tacit consent and the lorry, which had been leading, fell to the rear. Michael had all along been dubious of the mission; like Russell, but for different reasons, he was accustomed to giving such places a wide berth, and did not relish the idea of spending even a night in a mission compound. Missionaries are by no means universally admired in Africa, nor their activities approved of. From the point of view of the average Rhodesian, who is sensitive to any threat to white supremacy, they stir up a lot of trouble by giving the black man ideas above his station. They offer him education, which is a mistake; they teach him a few of the white man's habits, which is impertinent; and worst of all they treat him almost as an equal, calling him 'mister' on occasion and even shaking hands. To go into an area where such perversions were practised was enough to make Michael's hackles rise, and since we wished to make a friendly approach to the Chikore missionaries we hoped to keep him in the background as much as possible.

We drove gingerly along the paths of the mission, past open one-storey brick buildings which were evidently classrooms, past nondescript huts and bungalows and tennis-courts, wondering whom we should find to speak to and whom we should ask for advice and permission to camp. We drew up indecisively outside a small suburban-looking house with children's toys and tricycles in the garden, and almost at once fell over a pleasant, harassed and wispy young American woman with a baby. She directed us, without unseemly surprise, to the secondary school at the bottom of the hill. The superintendent of the mission was away that day, but we would find Mr Abbott, the headmaster, and he would take care of us.

It was necessary to move quickly now, for it was nearly five o'clock and in an hour it would be dark. We sought out Mr Abbott in his classroom, explained our needs and asked permission to camp, and after the briefest possible delay were setting up our tents on a cheerless and uncomfortable piece of ground which was the only one available. Short of accommodating us on the football ground or in one of the classrooms I do not know where else he could have put us, for the whole place was tidily laid out in approximate imitation of a campus; whereas here, on a sort of vacant lot among weeds and rubble, we had at least the vestiges of privacy, a sappy undergrowth screening us on one side, so that we could set up our transient arrangements without giving free entertainment to the populace. But it was not a nice camp, and the cook and Shorty sulked immediately. In the first place, there was no stream, so it was triumphantly announced that we could have no tea, and there could be no washing or cooking. Mr Abbott had said that we could take all the water we wanted from his outside tap, and we were only a few hundred yards away from his bungalow; but there were three dogs sitting on the Abbotts' back porch who barked very angrily indeed when they saw Shadow, and none of our boys would go near them. It was dark by the time the tents were up, and the cook was wandering about very slowly with his little gas-stove, complaining that there was no level ground where he could set it up, and that consequently there was no way of cooking dinner. Shorty had difficulty in finding wood for the fires, and when he did find some it was wet and would not burn. Everybody was tired and out of temper. Even Michael, whose good nature was unshakable and whose first thought was always to make an efficient camp, however difficult our eccentricities made it, leaned moodily smoking against the bonnet of the lorry, and we could see that for once he was on the Africans' side.

We did what we could, building up and fanning the reluctant fire against the night which already promised to be cold. We put on sweaters and drank some whisky, staring at the hissing logs and marvelling that one could so abruptly begin to shiver after the heat of the day. We were hungry now, and in sudden impatience with the cook's lamentations cut up a brace of guinea-fowl, already plucked and cleaned at the last camp, for Peter to roast over the heart of the fire on a piece of iron netting, heavy as a gridiron, which he had stumbled over in the hardware store in Chipinga and thought might come in useful. He is one of those men who pride themselves on their cooking, and if one is not too nice about his methods the results are often successful. It was so tonight. By the time he had seasoned and oiled the pieces of flesh the centre of the trench was glowing with red-hot ash, and they went on the hot gridiron with an audible sizzle. While we sat watching them change in colour and form, dropping their succulent juices on to the embers, the cook appeared out of the velvety dark and with silent disapproval laid a table. He set out knives and forks, bread, salt and pepper and butter, and a dish of cold baked beans in tomato as a neat but eloquent comment on the situation. He had from the first maintained that it was not correct to cook on an open fire, and that he would have nothing to do with it. When Peter had hopefully bought a round iron cooking-pot in Chipinga, the sort that is in universal use on African fires, he had grandly pretended not to know what it was, and had told us through John, the Zulu, who spoke some English, that he had always cooked in a hotel and was not accustomed to such things. But now the guinea-fowl were ready and we were ravenous, and cheerfully risked his silent disapproval. We ate with our fingers, sometimes holding the lightly charred bone in the corner of a handkerchief to avoid burning, and using the rest to mop the delicate juice which ran down our chins. We ate no bread and there was plenty of meat for the four of us, and I never remember a more satisfying meal. I do not know what the Africans ate: their staple diet was boiled mealie-meal which they squeezed into firm grey lumps the size of tennis-balls and dipped in gravy; but on this occasion, with no piece of ground level enough to suit the fanatical requirements of the gas-stove and the cook in a crisis of dignity, I suspect they dined poorly.

The night was unbelievably cold. We had discovered at Tanganda that we had been equipped with only a single blanket apiece, and Jack and I had bought a couple of gaudy African ones at Chipinga, for which we were now thankful. Peter was impervious to the cold, having sensibly brought a down-quilted sleeping-bag into which he retired each night like a wasp into its hole, and Michael slept on the ground in the open, so near the fire that he charred his blankets and clothes on several occasions, and in any case slept too soundly to feel anything; but Jack and I were pierced through and through with the cold, and my hip-bones ached and locked in a wrong position, as though a suicide's stake had been driven through my body.

At six o'clock, however, the African sun rose blazing out of the darkness, and in the same moment we heard the voices of children singing hymns. We got up without regret and thawed our bones. One could see by daylight, even more clearly than before, how comfortless was the spot that we were in, and we were glad to find that the boys were packing to leave. We had been offered baths at half-past six and breakfast at seven by the hospitable Abbotts, so leaving Michael to break camp and go on ahead (he had himself, to our relief, declined any closer acquaintance with the missionaries) we three went up to the Abbotts' comfortable bungalow, and for half an hour forgot the very reason for our expedition in the sensual pleasures of thick towels and unlimited hot water.

After breakfast (a delicious reminder of how wonderful fresh orange juice, fried eggs and American coffee can be) we were taken off to another bungalow to meet Chikore's missionary superintendent. He turned out, rather unexpectedly, to be young, good-looking and athletic, with crew-cut hair and an enthusiasm for Africa and its people which threw up a fountain of facts at the first approach; exactly, as Peter said afterwards, like striking a gusher. He was in love with his job, and with his marvellous luck in being here in Africa, and was saddened only by the fact that the gospel he had come to preach left singularly little mark on the African people. About ten per cent. of the boys and girls, he said, adopted a nominal Christianity while they were in school; after that one could not count on more than two per cent. Belief in magic and the fear of evil spirits were far deeper than any temporary love of God. They were avid for education, but did not want the pill inside the sugar; if they accepted it at first out of politeness they spat it out again as soon as they got home.

Both 'Chuck' Blakney, as he apparently was called, and Mr Abbott had been at pains to learn Chindau, the local language, and Mr Abbott in particular had a good detailed knowledge of the surrounding country, since there was a number of native village

schools in the area, taught by Chikore-trained teachers under the
guidance of the mission, and these had periodically to be visited.
The missionaries had good maps, and spread them out eagerly
on the floor for our inspection, but, as we expected, they all
went blank at the Rhodesian border, and beyond it could tell us
nothing. Still, it was probable that the missionaries themselves
could tell us much, and I cautiously began to ask them relevant
questions. It had already been explained at breakfast that our
choice of this part of the country for our trip was due to our
interest in the early adventures of my uncle, and our desire to
identify the places where he had been. They had eagerly asked
for his name and further details, and I told them as much as I
dared, not without a tremor of discomfort. I had the feeling that
if they had known the truth they would have disapproved of it,
and would have disapproved still more of our not telling it.
Still, I was determined to try them with a few place names from
Russell's narrative, and with studied carelessness asked them if
they had ever heard of the Longwegi River. After a considering
pause they shook their heads; then, pushing his forefinger doubtfully about the map, Chuck Blakney asked if the name might
not be a version of M'rongwezi. There was, he said, a considerable strain of Zulu blood in these people, and on either side
of the Portuguese border many rivers and natural features had
two names, one Chindau, one Zulu. A Chindau name beginning
with 'l' would in Zulu as likely as not begin with 'r', and the
apostrophized 'm' in M'rongwezi was so universal a characteristic that, in trying to identify a name, we could safely dis-
count it. We examined the map with bated breath and exchanged
glances. The M'rongwezi River was indeed where we had
supposed, from Russell's description, the Longwegi would be.
The letters 'g' and 'z', Blakney added, were also interchangeable
between the two languages, so that it seemed pretty certain that
this was the river my uncle had mentioned in his letters. In any
case, he said, if we were going that way he could give us an
introduction to a local chief, Zamchiya, who knew much more

about the native names than he did. If his guess about the river were right, the area we wanted to explore would be in Zamchiya's territory, and he might be able to give us a guide, for it was tricky country.

This seemed a marvellous step forward, and by tacit consent we mentioned no more names. We did not wish to pin-point our objective, for if Umgila's kraal and possibly Kyabanga were in this chief's territory, it was more than likely that he would know about the treasure, and would suspect us as soon as we mentioned these vital places. Our best plan would be to meet Zamchiya and proceed cautiously on any information which he was able to give us; we said we should be grateful for an introduction.

Mr Abbott now sat down to write a letter and to type out instructions for finding the chief's village, which was called by his name according to African custom, while Mr Blakney described the man on whom so much would depend. He was, he said, a remarkably fine person, a Christian, mission-educated, speaking quite good English, and was, so far as he knew, the only African chief to become a schoolmaster. He taught in the village school in Zamchiya, and administered territory on both sides of the Portuguese border. It was a long way off, and the roads—the two young men looked at each other and laughed. Well, at least we couldn't say that we hadn't been warned. We would find Zamchiya all right if the vehicles held out. If one of them broke, they said, we could always pile into the other and come back to Chikore.

In the moment of parting Mr Blakney showed us a further kindness which was to be more fruitful than he knew. Since I seemed interested in native history, he said, he would lend me a book which would tell me something about the people of Gazaland, the old name for the territory into which we were going. I could return it when we came back through Chikore, which we were almost bound to do. It was a pity we had not been able to stay longer, for there were some mysterious African ruins within reach of the mission which we might have cared to see. Most people, he said, had heard of Zimbabwe but had no idea that the country was dotted with remains of the same culture, which few white men had seen. They were hard to find and difficult to see, and we must not expect the natives to be eager to show them, since anything unknown was regarded with fear and they believed these places to be inhabited by powerful spirits. Right here, he said, returning to the map, right in the part where we were going, was a big hill, almost a mountain, called M'jenami, which certainly had some traces of African ruins, though nobody from Chikore had ever seen them. They had heard from other missionaries that they were there, and that except for these missionaries they were unknown to Europeans. If we found them, he said, he would like to hear about it, for one day he might be able to go into that country and see them for himself.

We promised we would do our best, and parted from our kind Americans with more gratitude than we could well convey. They had given us our first clue to Umgila's territory.

5

A Little Mutiny

As soon as we were out of sight of the mission we stopped the Land Rover and eagerly unfolded our maps. If Mr Blakney was right, and the M'rongwezi was the river we were looking for, we surely had only to follow its course eastward into Portuguese territory to find the site of Umgila's old village (if this were still visible), and from there strike a trail into the high veldt which might, or might not, bring us within range of Kyabanga. Russell's map had not been drawn to scale, and was no more than a scrawled memorandum; still, it was clear enough; the Longwegi, flowing from west to east, crossed the Rhodesian–

Portuguese border an unspecified number of miles north of the point where the Lundi and the Sabi became one, and turned their course eastward for the Indian Ocean. In some of our maps no river at all was shown which crossed the border; in one, such a river was clearly marked, but without a name. In our three War Office maps a river appeared in the right place, but so variously drawn as to look like three different rivers, and named Murongwezi, Morunguese and Mossurize—variants, one would say, of the M'rongwezi which had been carefully spelled out for me at the mission. It seemed to us then, as it seemed even more positively later, when we had learned more of the variations between Chindau and Zulu names and the fanciful divergences of maps, that the M'rongwezi was, indeed, Umgila's river, and that we were on Russell's trail and solid ground at last. Shorn of the prefix M', Mu- or Mo-, which is simply an attempt to introduce in writing a sound from a spoken language, Longwegi and Rongwezi are not very different: when one remembers that 'l' and 'r', and also 'g' and 'z', are interchangeable between Zulu and Chindau, they are seen to be the same.

We were elated by this confirmation of our hopes, which had been based on Peter's obsessional study of the dreadful maps (no two of which agreed, and which were becoming frayed as we snatched them fiercely from hand to hand) and calculated that, if we followed the missionaries' advice about our next camp, we should that very night be within reasonable distance of M'jenami, which seemed to lie slap across the international boundary and to command a view of the M'rongwezi River. M'jenami was suddenly of the greatest importance to us. From its summit we should get an open view of the surrounding country, and would be able to take bearings on any other hill that was to be seen. Once there, with Umgila's river in sight, we could not be many miles from Kyabanga.

There was another point about M'jenami which we saw at once could be turned to our advantage. The missionaries had said that there were mysterious Bantu ruins on the mountain, and these, surely, would give us the perfect excuse for camping in the vicinity and doing some otherwise inexplicable prowling. We were all the time nervously conscious of the necessity of convincing Michael that we were behaving normally; our Africans, too, as we had learned from him, were asking questions, and it was desirable that they should be satisfied about our motives, or they would talk; and we were also aware, as Russell had been before us, that we were never free from native observation. Four Europeans on safari, moving through country to which white men on safari never came, was altogether too rare and sensational an entertainment to be missed, and we quickly got used to the circumstance that as soon as we stopped anywhere, however briefly, an audience, usually children with goats and women with water-pots, would silently appear out of the bush. From every point of view this theory of Bantu ruins was a godsend, and we worked up a by no means altogether false enthusiasm for them as we bumped and lurched over the execrable road which would bring us to Mariya.

This was the spot at which we had agreed to meet Michael, having sent him ahead with the lorry to look for a suitable camping place in the vicinity while we stayed to collect information from the missionaries. They had told us that there was a village school at Mariya, which we could hardly miss, and also a bore-hole with good water. We had arranged to meet there, at the school, at noon, and followed the atrocious road with rising spirits, buoyed up by the belief that if we made a convenient camp near Mariya we should be within a few miles of our objective. Alas for our hopes, we had not allowed for the unpredictability of Michael, and were about to run into a series of maddening difficulties.

At first the road wound through steep and rocky woodlands, and we crossed the River Nyangadza, which had plenty of water in it, three times, always at shallow fords which were easily negotiable. The road was punitively bad, but we had seen nothing yet. Presently it dropped down out of the hills into flat bush and native farming country, and became ridged and hard-baked track which had never been made for vehicles at all but had been worn through the bush by the feet of men and animals. It was a featureless landscape now, and all the streams were dry. We came to Mariya about noon, and found it to be a collection of shed-like brick buildings, evidently classrooms, circled about with a number of native huts. The bore-hole, a deep well worked by a primitive hand-pump, was under a shelter of thatch a little distance from the road, and there was a busy traffic of women, children and goats threading their way through the grass in every direction. The air was full of dust and the sun fierce, and to find a margin of shade we had to run the Land Rover under the open front of one of the classrooms. There was no question of finding a more comfortable spot, if we were not to run the risk of missing Michael, and since school seemed to be over for the day we took our books into the empty shelter and settled down to wait.

It was a fairly dirty place, open down the whole length of one side like a cart-shed and furnished with a few rough tables and benches which had been made by fixing legs here and there to the split trunks of trees. It contained nothing else whatever except excrement in the corners and a universal covering of dust. We sat on the benches and read for four hours, denied even the comfort of the Land Rover since the sun had found it at last and the only shade was under the classroom roof.

The non-appearance of Michael was certainly worrying, but we comforted ourselves with the news, politely offered in English by the African school-teacher, that a big blue lorry driven by a European had gone through Mariya that morning without stopping. At least we were all headed in the same direction, and we supposed that he would be back in his own good time if nothing had gone wrong with the lorry. The hours of waiting, too, were not wholly wasted, for I had time to look through the book Mr Blakney had lent me, and in it found information which seemed unexpectedly to confirm Russell's story.

At the beginning of his narrative Russell had given the name of the buried chief as 'Umgila or Langilibilele', and had said that his son Gungunyana had had trouble with the Portuguese, and that as a result of this trouble the old kraal had been deserted and the people scattered. I had pricked up my ears at Chikore when Mrs Abbott, over breakfast, speaking of Mount Selinda, had said that an important chief called Gungunyana was said to be buried in the precincts, though nobody knew where, for this suggested that there was still some living memory of Umgila's son, and not so very far from his father's country. Now, turning the leaves of this excellent book, *The Life of a South African Tribe* by Henri A. Junod, in one of the historical chapters I came across a paragraph about a Zulu chief, Muzila, who had been defeated in a war of succession with his brother, had moved with his followers to Gazaland, and been eventually succeeded by his son, Gungunyana. There was very little about him, but the paragraph stood up suddenly from the page as though it were magnified. Surely, surely, this was our very man? The names Muzila and Umgila were clearly variants of one name, '*mu*', 'Um' or 'M' being the prefix and the 'z' and 'g' interchangeable according to whether it were spoken in Zulu or Chindau. There was one other detail, which might or might not be relevant. The paragraph mentioned 'his capital, Mandla-kasi', and we wondered whether this might refer to the abandoned village, where Russell had first dug, or perhaps to the one he passed on the border as he crossed into Portuguese territory, mentioned by him in the narrative as 'Mandhalami's kraal'. It would be unwise to lay too much stress on this last similarity, since we were ignorant of the language, but we felt sure that the book's Muzila was our Umgila, and we set great store by this casual historical reference, for it convinced us that Russell's chief had really existed, and in that part of the country where we had hoped to find him.

By four o'clock it seemed depressingly likely that something had happened to Michael, and that since it would be totally dark by six we had better make preparations for spending the night. We asked permission of the school-teacher, whose name was Abel, and who seemed glad of an opportunity of practising his English. He offered us the classroom to sleep in, and threw some sticks on the fire outside his hut so that we could boil our kettle. We had nothing with us but some tea, a tin of milk and some Ryvita, and were getting hungry, so it seemed sensible that Peter and I should go back to the last native store we had passed to buy some bully-beef and bananas, two staples which, together with Coca-Cola, can be found in the meanest native store in Africa. This store had been mentioned to us by the missionaries since, though a poor little store in itself and not very clean, it was owned by a successful African farmer called Hla-Hla, one of the big men of the neighbourhood, whom we came to know and appreciate some time later. We did not see him on this occasion but got what we wanted from the storekeeper and crashed our way back over the trail in a hurry, not liking the idea of finding our way in the dark.

When we got back to Mariya the big blue lorry was breathing its diesel rhythm in the middle of the road and Michael and Jack were examining a map by the light of an electric torch. Even as we came up to them, probing with our headlights across the ruts and stones, the sunless twilight faded like a theatrical effect and darkness took its place, broken only by our headlamps and the red glow of the school-teacher's cooking fire. The bad news was broken without delay. Michael was so late because he had gone another twenty miles farther south, and had made camp on the first river he had found with water in it. This was the Honde, a long way from where we wanted to be, and at the sight of our blank faces he said he could see no good reason for our wanting to be nearer to Mariya. It was no use arguing; the camp was made, and for tonight at least there was nothing to do but to go to it. Not for one night but two, Michael insisted; the *munts* were acting sullen at having to break camp so often, and we had better stay put for a while if we wanted to avoid trouble.

He had gone so far because all the rivers were dry, and he had had to go all that distance for a running river. We wanted water in our camp, didn't we? He seemed surprised that we received all his reasonable arguments so dejectedly.

We decided to split up two and two, as the road was going to be difficult in the dark. Michael and Jack went ahead in the lorry and Peter and I followed in the Land Rover in a cloud of choking, reddish, impenetrable dust. There seemed to be no way of avoiding this; if we dropped behind to let it subside we immediately lost the lights of the lorry and found ourselves crashing and lurching through the long grass among the scrub and without any clue to our direction. Even attempting to keep up, and staying within the dust-storm which was our guide, we missed the lorry's lights on several occasions, and each time lost all sense of being on a road. Head thrust out of the side window as we pitched shatteringly from hole to hole, Peter would shout furiously, 'I don't believe this is a road we're on at all!' I would open my window for a moment for a better view, holding my breath against the dust. 'I believe you're right. It does seem much more like a ditch.' More crashing and lurching and crawling over boulders. 'Good God, I know what it is, it's a dried-up water-course!' He stopped at this and got out to have a look, and after a moment's hesitation I got out too, jumping down in the dark into an invisible bush which clasped me in a barbed-wire embrace and ran delicate three-inch thorns into my flesh. We had lost the lorry's lights by this time, but there was nothing to do but go on. Even on foot the twenty miles could scarcely have seemed longer, and the groan of the Land Rover's four-wheel drive made a bassoon accompaniment to the rattles and crashes of our belongings as we bounced in the air and were hurled at the metal sides. After a time Peter shouted above the din with regained confidence, 'I believe it's a road after all! I saw the lorry's lights,' and there they were, sending a faint glimmer through the dust and trees a hundred yards ahead. Encouraged, he trod cautiously on the accelerator, and we struck a rock with such force that we came to a shocked standstill, straining and shuddering like a ship aground. We were properly stuck this time; the rock was under the body of the Land Rover, supporting it like a pedestal while the wheels spun and made grooves in the hard soil. I scarcely know how we got her off again: I took the wheel and roared the engine while Peter pushed, and after some agonizing minutes their combined strength succeeded in slipping her sideways. Speechless with temper, Peter climbed in again, his clothes filthy and his face unrecognizable under a coating of cinnamon-coloured dust.

It seemed a high price to pay for getting to a place where we had no wish to be, and when we arrived at the camp we saw nothing to make us like it any better. The Honde River, for which we had made this lengthy and damaging detour, proved to be a miserable trickle among stones with stagnant, unwholesome-looking pools here and there; the perfect breeding-ground, one would say, for bilharzia. The patch of open ground, where our tents were already set, was bald and uninviting, littered with the blackened relics of old fires, with rusty wire and pieces of dirty newspaper. The tsetse-fly control, it appeared, had camped here the year before, and had left these souvenirs of their occupation. There were no trees of any size, so that we could see at a glance that there would be no shade, and the camp was surrounded by long rustling grass which Michael had already found to be full of snakes. He had shot a fine black mamba while the tents were going up, and had seen another which had eluded him; he showed us the tattered trophy of his kill and flung it into the bushes.

We shuffled about in the darkness, dragging our immediate needs out of the Land Rover, depressed by the wretched change in our situation. The mantle of the gas-lamp had naturally shattered on the journey and no spare had been provided. There was only one battered storm-lantern, which the cook needed. He had used up all the Calor gas already and the refrigerator had gone wrong. We gloomily thanked Heaven we had thought to bring a private packet of candles, which at least would give us light for going to bed; for the rest we must make do with fire-light.

After all the optimism of the morning our prospects had maddeningly deteriorated. We were now a good twenty miles from our objective and almost as far from the long southernmost spur of M'jenami, which we had fixed on as our next centre of operations. We were cut off from the area of search by hours of slow going over an execrable trail, and were uneasy about the damage done to the Land Rover. Worst of all, we were con-demned to this hateful place for two nights, for Michael was firm that the boys must have a rest from moving camp, or we should run into trouble.

All this was discouraging enough, but when the night was over and the hot sun stinging our arms as we surveyed the sordid confusion of our camp, we were visited by new and irritable energy and determined to get back where we wanted to be, no matter how unpopular it made us. It was no good staying here, we told Michael. We were too far south for the country connected with my uncle, and had heard, besides, some interest-ing news of ruins from the missionaries, which made us anxious to explore M'jenami. We had not thought, we said, to mention before that my uncle had been particularly interested in Bantu ruins, and had described them in his letters to my mother. We could not let this opportunity pass, and therefore proposed to spend the day in looking for a good base-camp farther north, where we could stay for several days while we explored the mountain. Michael, on the other hand, was all for pressing farther south, to Hippo Mine, where he had heard the game was plentiful and thought he knew the tsetse-fly officer. This chap would be shooting out the game and it would be fun to help him; it could not, he thought, be more than a day's journey. The argument was developed during breakfast, interrupted only by the sudden appearance of a long and extremely beautiful green mamba pouring smoothly out of the grass at the side of the meat-safe. The boys scattered shrieking and climbed into the lorry, while Michael, never so happy as with his finger on a trigger, pursued it keenly but fruitlessly into the grass. We took advantage of his momentary absence to think of a few more reasons why we could not do as he suggested, and when he returned we were civilly but resolutely firm. We three would go off for the day and look around, and find a better camp site if possible.

Retraced by daylight, the trail was less alarming than it had been in the dark, but it was bad enough, and we were horrified to see the rock on which we had foundered. It was a sort of flat-headed crag jutting out of the ground, cracked and scored in evidence of our passage. So far as Peter had been able to discover, the Land Rover had not been dangerously damaged, but one of the track-rods was buckled and the steering was heavy. He began to wonder lugubriously where was the nearest point where repairs were possible. It was just conceivable that Mr Hla-Hla, the great man who had a grinding-mill, a tractor and a lorry, might also have a repair workshop; if he had not, it might mean going all the way back to Chikore, for we could not risk a breakdown later on, when much might depend on our mobility, in conditions still unknown across the border.

It was, as usual, a morning so marvellous that it might have been the beginning of the world. Now that we could see where we were going, we found the endless sameness of the bush confusing; long grass and low trees, dappled with sun and shade, shut in the trail on every side, so that one could not see more than a score of yards in any direction. The trail meandered where it pleased, sometimes dividing for no apparent reason and coming together again after a quarter of a mile, sometimes forking off in divergent directions, with small possibility of knowing which was right. Left to myself I should have been soon lost, having a poor sense of direction and an incomplete grasp of the proper use of the compass; but we did not lose our way; Jack and Peter read their inadequate maps, paid attention to the position of the sun, and sometimes climbed on to the roof of the Land Rover to look for natural features predicted by the maps which were occasionally, but by no means always, there. We were beset by a thirst so fierce that there was no accounting for it by anything we had eaten, and stopped every few miles to drink greedily from our tepid water-bottles. We came to the conclusion after several hours that this was due simply to the stinging heat, to which we were not yet accustomed, and which made the roof of the Land Rover too hot to touch; even with the windows and the draught-vent open it was rather like travelling in a portable oven.

We reached Mariya before noon, and finding the school in session, with scores of little black heads in the classrooms and a loud chanting of multiplication tables going on, took the only alternative trail which branched to the west, hoping to find the second bore-hole of which the missionaries had spoken. These bore-holes* were a Government enterprise, designed to make country habitable which could not otherwise support life in the dry season, and they told us that the one at Chimedzi was even better than the busy one at Mariya, since the water came up from the greensand and could be drunk without boiling. Chimedzi lay five miles to the west of Mariya, and though there was no village or visible habitation we found the bore-hole easily, its wooden pump-handle protected from the sun by a thatched shelter and the surrounding dust churned into chocolate-coloured mud by the feet of men and cattle. We were now in gentle wooded country where the trees grew almost to forest size and there were dramatic rocks. Some miles away on our left we had seen a tremendous escarpment, its flank clothed with some sort of scrub and its edge crowned with serrated rock which in the distance and the dazzling light looked extraordinarily like archi-

---

* The two we saw were simple pipes sunk to the permanent water-table and operated by a primitive hand-pump. There had been great resistance on the part of the natives to using them, but gradually the dwellers in these seasonally dry areas had become reconciled, though many of the women habitually walked as many as fourteen miles a day for a running stream, fetching the day's supply in waterpots.

tecture. At each point where the ground rose sufficiently to give us another view of it the illusion became stronger, until we were impelled to stop and get out the field-glasses. To the naked eye it looked now like a little town, and the glasses encouraged the *trompe-l'œil*, for the rocks were regular and cubiform with slate-coloured tops, arranged like a seaside crescent and looking like nothing so much as Victorian boarding-houses. All that was wanting was the flash of windows.

About six miles from this extraordinary feature and less than two from the Chimedzi bore-hole we found what seemed to us a perfect camping place, on gently sloping ground splendidly shaded by trees and under the lee of some small wooded crags. These too would give us shade in the afternoon; there seemed to be no native village anywhere near and it was very peaceful. We lit a fire and made coffee under the trees and ate our lunch of bully-beef and Ryvita, which experience had now reduced to a ritual of the utmost simplicity. The Ryvita would be dealt in rotation like cards, then the tin would be opened and passed from hand to hand and the meat dug out with clasp-knives and laid on the biscuits. There was not much washing-up after such a meal; the knives could be cleaned by plunging them into the ground and our enamel mugs rinsed at the bore-hole later. It was delicious to lie back afterwards in the shade and sleep, lulled by the crooning of the small doves which seem to inhabit every grove in Africa, undisturbed by the quiet rustling which by this time we knew to be made by little black boys appearing as usual like spirits out of the bush.

We returned to the Honde camp in high feather, delighted with our success, for our new place, as near as we could calculate, was only twelve or fifteen miles from the M'rongwezi and within easy reach of M'jenami, while the splendid trees and the bore-hole would give us both shade and water. We were dismayed, however, to meet a blandly discouraging response from Michael. It was all very well for us, he said, but the *munts* would not go to another camp where there was no river. They did not count wells and bore-holes and would not use them; there must be a river into which they could plunge to wash themselves and their clothes, and where John could do the laundry. It was their invariable custom; they thought it unspeakably dirty to wash in bowls, and it was no good expecting them to change their habits. He saw the point, he said; a river was essential; the obvious thing was to move twenty miles farther west and camp on the Sabi. The M'rongwezi, being in this area, was probably dry, but the Sabi was immense and never failed. There would be plenty to shoot there, he added wistfully. We should all enjoy it.

Always a weakling in argument, and now feeling the additional discomfort of a bad conscience, since Michael's transparent friendliness had made me fond of him and it felt uneasy not to be telling him the truth, I withdrew into my stifling tent and lay on the bed, leaving it to the others to convince him. They succeeded soon enough by their own methods, Peter being a forceful exponent of his own opinions and Jack persuasive, and it was settled at last that we should move in the morning. The boys had been soothed by the promise that we should settle for several days in the new camp, and that Michael, to whom continuous restless exertion was a necessity, should take them every second day to the Sabi River. This had disposed, we thought, of all their grievances, but it now transpired that the cook had developed another. On a proper safari, he said, the minimum provision was one African servant to one European; there were four of us and only three of them, and therefore (he did not put it in quite these words but this was the gist of his thesis) the balance of nature was disturbed. Moreover, he himself could not properly be counted as one of the three, since his sole province was the kitchen, and he should not be asked to help in moving camp. And one final point: he should correctly be addressed as 'Chef', and not as 'Cook'.

Michael strode away from him without answering, his face pink and his Rhodesian hackles rising. His own solution, he told us, would be to give him a hiding, but in deference to our

feelings, and at some sacrifice of bossmanship, he would overlook
the bastard's cheek this once and try to think of some workable
arrangement. The cook was a city *munt*, a soft *munt*; he had
never been on safari in his life; it had been a great mistake to
bring him. The trouble was, the only other applicant for the job,
though a better cook and used to the bush, had been a known
thief, and Michael's father had been reluctant to employ him.
With John, the Zulu, there was never any trouble; he and
Michael respected one another. John was twenty-four, a
married man and a Christian; he had sent his second wife back
to her father after his conversion. He was gentle in manner and
speech and never out of temper; he rarely took part in the others'
quarrels, but was usually to be seen smiling at a little distance,
hanging out clothes or ironing Michael's shirts on top of the
meat-safe.

Shorty was a different character altogether. Thirty-two and
coal-black, he was unmarried, cheerful, and a known menace to
women. His legs were abnormally short but he was very
powerful, and could drag whole tree-trunks up to the fire which
even Peter or Michael would have despaired of lifting. He was
vain of his appearance, and was always avid for pieces of cast-off
clothing. His chief pride was a chauffeur's cap, ornamented in
the front with a free-advertisement badge saying 'O.K. Cigar-
ettes'; with this he wore broken sand-shoes, khaki shorts and a
series of vests and sleeveless shirts in every conceivable stage of
dissolution. He was hard on his clothes, and Michael had some
difficulty in keeping him provided. We all of us in time contri-
buted to his wardrobe, and he rang the changes on a bizarre
collection of garments, usually split like a grin after a few days'
wear, exposing his shoulder-blades and jaunty buttocks. I never
saw anyone else who could so freely express his feelings by his
walk. He set off on his forays after the girls strutting like a
cockerel, and after a hearty swearing-at by Michael would move
away from the scene of the scolding slowly, moving his buttocks
with a provocative jerk which was the very epitome of dumb

insolence. But he was a friendly character and bore no grudges, and often gave Michael as good as he got, dodging his hand or boot with a flashing grin and enjoying the ready wit of his own impudence. We became rather fond of Shorty, who was one of nature's clowns and a cheerful sinner. He knew what sin was, and greatly enjoyed it, being a member—who would have guessed it?—of the Dutch Reformed Church.

The cook was like neither of these, being a morose character with a sense of his own importance, and a permanent grievance due to the fact that he genuinely felt he had been cheated. He had never been on safari before but had heard great things about it, and I suspect he had calculated that it would enhance his prestige to have been on an expedition with Europeans. He had dressed for the part, and the part had folded under him. There were no elaborate camps and no finger-bowls; no big game had been shot, he had not been addressed as 'Chef', and he had done a lot of hard travelling. Now he found himself many miles from home, in a harsh and burnt-up country where the rivers were dry, at the mercy of people who had insulted him twice by cooking their food themselves, and who had known no better than to buy him a kaffir-pot. It was too much. He ceased to wear his chef's outfit as a protest, and though he took some part in the work of moving camp he made it clear that he lowered himself unwillingly.

The crisis came at Chimedzi, as soon as the camp was made, when John had carried the luggage and made the beds and Shorty had dug two trenches and got two fires blazing, and the two of them with Michael in the lorry had taken two empty paraffin-drums to the bore-hole and fetched water. As darkness fell we had heard some unpleasant snickering laughter in the rocks above us, and had thought that as usual we had attracted an audience, as indeed we had; but it was not boys this time, it was hyenas; and this was the straw which broke the cook's resistance. He downed tools in tears, vowing that he was going home in the morning unless he were promised four pounds above his contract and a present at the end of it, and retired to sulk under a piece of tarpaulin.

We received this ultimatum with some callousness, not seeing how he was to carry out this threat without walking alone for several days through the bush; besides, we were tired of his tantrums, and felt it was preferable to live on bully-beef for ever rather than endure them. So we ate out of tins and ignored him, and John washed up in water that stank of paraffin. (Our camping in a place where water was fifteen minutes by lorry had revealed yet another gap in our equipment: the canvas water-bags on our list proved to be only one, and that a small one, so that every journey yielded only half a gallon.)

It was a warm and marvellously beautiful night, quite dark except for the stars, which streamed like phosphorescence in a deep sea and, as the fire dwindled, shed a ghostly brilliance. I decided to sleep out. Even on cold nights I had found the tent oppressive, and now Jack, who had a sore throat and was feeling vaguely unwell, had taken to snoring on a scale that made sleep within a couple of feet of him impossible. I dragged my bed out, and Michael helped me to carry it to the fire. He had given up the use of a bed himself, preferring to scoop out a hollow in the ground and get into it with his blankets. Certainly our camp-beds were particularly torturous, and mine, as well as having a wooden cross-bar at the exact point where a bed is bound to receive the human hip, had a habit of kneeling down in the night like a camel. Still, the pleasure of lying out under those stars, with the fire's glowing trench warming the blankets and the leaves curling with heat a great distance above, was so exquisite that discomfort soon faded and one sank into sleep on waves of dream-like contentment.

I was wakened suddenly, after a long time it seemed, by a stealthy rustling in the bushes behind my bed. I lifted my head and listened, a tremor of shock rippling over my skin. It was very dark, for the fire had died down and was no more than a trough of faintly glowing ash. I could just make out Michael, prone as a log on the other side, his head under the blankets, obviously fast asleep. From the two tents, a good way off, came rising and falling cadences of snoring. Nobody else had stirred. After a brief silence it came again, and my tingling senses told me it was nearer. Something was moving cautiously in the thicket, in the thorny tangle that lay between my bed and the foot of the rocks. I called to Michael. There was no response. After a shiver of indecision I got out of bed and shook him vigorously by the feet, which were sticking up oddly under his grey blanket. Still he did not stir. I grasped his shoulder, shouting in his ear; but all he did was to make some childish sounds and turn over in his sleep, for all the world like the Flopsy Bunnies when Mr McGregor was putting them into his sack. I had never known anybody sleep like this except a child, and I stood still with dismay at the realization that, short of pouring a bucket of water over him or pulling off the bedclothes, Michael was unwakable.

There was no question of crossing the open ground to either of the tents, so I got hurriedly back into bed, visited momentarily by that old panic of childhood in which one's legs feel morbidly vulnerable in the dark. No sooner had I done so than a figure came silently padding out of the blackness, ears pricked, muzzle seriously intent. It was Shadow doing his night-long round of the camp and pausing to investigate my disturbance. He stared into the bushes for a moment, then turned away with an eloquent lack of interest that told me plainly enough I need not have bothered. Some small nocturnal animal, some hungry kaffir dog scavenging for food, was all it was, and Shadow's expression, as he laid his muzzle momentarily on my pillow, was tolerant. He did not stay, but went off again on his silent reconnaissance.

I saw now that he was an invaluable member of our company, and that we need have no fear of night alarms while he was with us. He slept little during the hours of darkness: he always lay down with Michael at bedtime but was rarely there if one woke during the night, being seen only at intervals, making his stealthy rounds on the outskirts of the camp or sitting alert and aloof at a little distance. Michael assured us that no animal would approach the camp while Shadow was there, and he operated the same system against Africans during the day. It was his delight to go bounding through the bush after little boys, sending them mad with terror and stopping only reluctantly and at the last moment when Michael yelled at him. When we asked if he always gave up at the word of command Michael said, 'Well . . . usually,' leaving us with the feeling that there had been a few enjoyable sporting incidents. Both by training and temperament Shadow was an uncompromising Rhodesian.

6

M'jenami

BEFORE sunrise the little doves inhabiting all the trees and rocks of Chimedzi would begin their rhythmic day-long conversations, and I would get stiffly out of bed and mend the fire, dragging together the heavy logs that had burned through in the night and blowing the ash until I could boil a kettle. While the water heated I crouched beside the blaze, shivering in spite of my flannel pyjamas, warming the teapot and trying to distinguish between the musical phrases. The Chimedzi doves had three, and I was never able to discover whether these were different sentences, so to speak, or the characteristic calls of separate species. The opening statement, sleepily murmured at the first hint of light, was in three syllables, with a soft stress in the middle. It sounded as though they were calling 'm'*faz*-i, m'*faz*-i, m'*faz*-i' over and over again, a word I heard often in jesting conversations between Michael and Shorty and which was Shona for 'woman'. Michael was particularly fond of a story about one of the African boys on his father's farm, who had asked for an advance of a pound above his wages because he wanted an *m'fazi*. The average bride-price being anything up to thirty pounds, Michael's father had suggested that he wouldn't get much of a bride for only one, to which the reply had been, 'That's all right, boss, she very second-hand.' Now it seemed that the doves were all calling for their brides, and the bush was alive with the gentle amorous rhythm. Presently another statement would be made, still in three syllables but with the stress shifted. 'Kroo-kroo-*kroo* . . . kroo-kroo-*kroo*,' they were saying now, as though developing the theme, or perhaps starting a different one, a second movement. Before that was quite finished a third would begin, this time in four syllables and very emphatic; I could find no words to fit it except the prosaic injunction: 'Take the *Ro*-ver,' to which the lovely call had a ludicrous resemblance; and by the time I had made the tea and carried cups to Michael and the two tents this insistent invitation would be sounding from massed choirs all over the woods. I have since heard it reproduced in speech as 'Kroo, who *are* you? Kroo, who *are* you?' and have been told that this is the call of the Mourning Dove, found all over Africa; but it never struck me at the time as at all sad, only infinitely gentle and affectionate. There were other birds at Chimedzi, in particular a long ungainly hornbill which sailed about the crags like a glider but always landed in an unbalanced fashion, as though performing this operation for the first time; but we knew none of them by name, and Michael when asked could only say that they were crows. He would have made a fine gamekeeper, having the instinct to shoot at anything that moved; when his gun was not to hand, which was seldom, he would throw up his arm at any bird and take a sight along a finger.

Our first necessity, now that we were settled within reach of Umgila's territory, was to make certain of our position on the map, and to take bearings. The map showed a hill called Lusongo about six miles away, which we hoped would be the rocky escarpment we had examined through the glasses; but of this we could not be certain, for natives questioned at the bore-hole said it was Chitopa, and shook their heads when we mentioned the other name. If it *were* Lusongo, it was nearly two thousand feet above sea level, and according to the map had a survey beacon on top. Since we were already at an altitude of about fifteen hundred this would make the height of the feature about four or five hundred feet, which seemed right; but there was no way of being certain except to climb it. We had had a good look at it from the top of our own crags, and had again marvelled at the architectural illusion of its summit, which varied according to the light between a uniform row of houses and a noble ruin.

After one or two false starts, following promising-looking trails through the high grass which ended at a mealie-patch, we brought the Land Rover to the foot of the ascent and left it under the shade of a giant boulder. The hill was almost as steep as a cliff, and the grassy gullies by which we climbed were full of thorn bushes, the now familiar 'wait-a-bit thorn' which is such an excruciating expert in delay, but we scrambled up slowly, Peter leading, clapping his hands smartly to discourage snakes. When we reached the top and came out on the very crags we had seen from Chimedzi, the sweat was running into my eyes so that I could scarcely see; but as our breathing quietened and we sat on the warm rocks in a welcome breeze, we slowly took in a view of some magnificence.

Lusongo—for so it proved to be, having a miniature cement obelisk stuck on its summit, marked with its name and altitude—was a huge rocky pile shaped on one face like a fortress and commanding a sweep of country which stretched in monotonous levels to the horizon. Only to the north-east, perhaps five miles away, was there a break in the monotony: a wooded hill shaped like a stranded mastodon, not high enough to be called a mountain but craggy and steep and about seven miles long, which map and compass confirmed as M'jenami. Beyond it was the first faint outline of what might have been further hills, too far off in the heat-hazed distance to be more than a supposition. This was the direction, according to Russell's map, in which Kyabanga and the high veldt lay, and we guessed that from M'jenami we should be able to get a clear idea of this farther country. To climb M'jenami, then, was our next target, and we gazed at it through the glasses with an illogical prophetic feeling that it was bound to yield us some essential clue. We would make an immediate attempt to search for ruins, and under cover of the search see if we could not discover something to our purpose. The missionaries had told us we should need a guide, and this we saw was essential, for apart from the fact that we might as well see the ruins while we were about it, we had learned enough to know that on a bush-covered seven-mile hill it would be only too easy to be lost.

We put our plans to Michael when we returned to camp, and found that he had spent the morning bargaining for another goat, this being his sovereign device for keeping the *munts* happy; a scraggy animal had already been shot and skinned and partially committed to the pot. The cook, with an air of melancholy grandeur, had announced that he would stay, and was already peeling onions and preparing to astonish us with a curry. Michael obligingly went off to Mariya to ask the school-teacher for a guide, and for an extra camp-boy if one were available. The grievances of the last few days seemed all to have evaporated, and with the smell of cooking and with John and Shorty full of smiles the camp had quite an atmosphere of festivity. There was, indeed, to be a beer-drinking that night in the near-by village, to which they were all invited, and the promise of a party had cheered them up like magic. We had seen no sign of a village when we came to Chimedzi, but had nevertheless discovered that the woods were thickly populated, and from the top of our own crags, with the field-glasses, had been able to distinguish a score of native huts, their thatch the same dry colour as the trees and to the naked eye quite invisible.

That night we sat round a fire of huge dimensions and ate a curry which really earned the repentant cook his title. We sent

seven o'clock we were
ting down to breakfast

ty . . . unmarried, cheer-
and a known menace to
women

It was wonderful to spend
the next day doing nothing

Peter . . . took sights a
calculated distances

A girl arrived in the camp . . . bearing on her
head a great pot of wild honey

He was not pleased
to see us

The blows of the pick could
have been heard a mile off

appreciative compliments to the chef, who came into the circle of firelight and bowed gravely. All was well. Already the drums were warming up for the beer-drinking, and Michael had returned with the promise of a guide for the morning. No difficulty had been made; the guide had said he knew the ruins well, and would come at first light and take us to them. We could hear little snatches of singing coming from a distance, and as the night wore on the drums became louder and gayer, rumbling and thumping in a variety of rhythms, with bursts of sociable shouting and women's laughter. Our boys had been given a shilling or two apiece as a contribution to the beer-making, and the cook had unbent so far as to brew a little himself in the kaffir-pot, maturing it by some private process during the afternoon. They returned in the small hours, falling over the washing-up bowl in the dark and giggling like children. The drums were still going, thumping and vibrating contrapuntally; each time a blessed silence fell another would begin; they did not die away till nearly six o'clock, when it was broad day.

At seven we were ready for our guide, but he did not come. The dawn chorus of the doves was over, and a brooding quiet had settled over the bush. Shorty was half-awake but unable to stand, so John was sent off to the bore-hole to make inquiries. He came back with the polite message that the guide was very sorry, he had broken his leg. This, Michael said, could mean anything. It could probably be interpreted as a hangover; or it could equally well be that he was afraid of the ruins and had no intention of showing them to Europeans. Michael sent a sharp message to the local headman; and this in time produced two old men with sacks over their shoulders, recommended by the headman as reliable and said to be conversant with the ruins. Hands on hips, with Shadow in attendance, he questioned them in Shona.

'Do you know any ruins on M'jenami?'

'Yes, boss.'

'If we take you to the foot of the mountain in the lorry, can you find the trail?'

D

'Yes, boss.'

'Will you take us there today?'

'No, boss.'

'Why not?''

The old men grinned and looked at one another.

'The wind blew them away.'

It was hopeless. Michael by this time had become infected with our determination, and went off in the lorry to see the headman himself. He came back looking triumphant, with a sober-looking elderly man with pierced ear-lobes who said he would willingly act as guide for a few shillings. He knew the ruins well, there was no difficulty.

We provisioned ourselves with bully-beef and coffee-making equipment, taking Michael as interpreter and Shorty with mattock and *panga*, the long-bladed African knife essential for slashing a way through dense growth, and set off in the Land Rover for M'jenami. We followed the old dreadful trail to the south, which had given us so much trouble in the dark, but only for several miles, stopping at a point which, in our need to refer to places which had no names, we privately thought of as 'the baboon village'. There was no village there, only a few tattered mealie-patches which were already harvested, but it must have been much frequented by baboons, for it was dotted about with those small thatched shelters in which boys are set on guard in the growing season to scare the baboons away with stones and shouting. We were now in a shallow valley, with gently rising ground on either side. To our right, less than a mile away, was one of the rocky faces of Lusongo. On our left, not yet steep but with the promise of heights to come, was what we knew must be the base of M'jenami. The grass was head-high and very thick; there was no sign of a trail.

Our guide now surprised us by strongly urging that we should climb not M'jenami but Lusongo, where, he said, the ruins were much larger and had, moreover, been built by Europeans. This was suspicious. We had already climbed Lusongo, and were pretty certain they were only illusory ruins on that extra-ordinary rock. This was carefully translated to our guide, who shook his head. Not only were there ruins, he said seriously, but also a cave furnished for habitation, with chairs and tables and even cooking pots. We exchanged glances. We had indeed seen a cave on the day we climbed Lusongo, containing the ashes of an old fire and an empty cigarette packet, and had supposed that they were the spoor of the Survey Department when they had been erecting the survey mark a few years before. The men had undoubtedly camped in the cave, and must at some time have used cooking equipment. Was it possible he thought we wished to see such a place, or that it held any interest?

We explained, through Michael, that we did not care for European remains, but only for those on M'jenami, which were said to be African. If he did not know those ruins he must say so, and we would look for ourselves. Oh, he knew them well, he said. They were much inferior to the ruins on Lusongo, but if that was what we wished to see he would take us to it. There was no path; if we had made up our minds, this was the point from which we should have to walk.

He turned resignedly into the long grass and we followed him, parting the feathery fronds with our hands and leaving behind a crushed and narrow trail. The sun was very hot, and we were glad when we came into the chequered shade of trees, for here the grass was mysteriously cool and we could feel the dew. We walked for several miles in this way, always on gently rising ground, skirting patches of mealie and millet here and there and occasionally passing small impermanent-looking huts, each one the nucleus of a primitive small-holding. At each hut we came to our guide paused, and if anyone were within, held a lengthy conference. From one of them eventually he recruited two more men, who regarded us unsmilingly but seemed to come willingly enough, nodding their heads and pointing pur-posefully upwards.

From this point the going was steep and rocky and we began to climb, strung out in a long Indian file of which I was the last and slowest member. The grass was still so high that I often lost sight of the others, and would scramble out of the holes into which I fell with the anxious feeling that if I paused my absence would not be noticed until they reached the summit. Breathing heavily, we came at last to the top of a ridge, and stopped to look about us. There was nothing to be seen yet but grass and trees, both just high enough to prevent our getting a view of anything else, and we stood round our guide inquiringly. Questioned by Michael, he now said he did not *precisely* know where the ruins were, but if we fanned out across the top we should surely find them. This we did, glad of the relief of having no farther to climb, and shouting from time to time to keep in touch. Presently the word came down the line that our guide remembered now, the ruins were on the next hill, which had just come into sight through a gap in the trees, separated from where we stood by a deep col. It now became apparent that the mountain was not the simple feature it had appeared to be, but a complex of successive ridges each higher than the last, culminating in a formidable cluster of naked crags. Like the summit of Lusongo, these crags had an architectural quality, as though they had been partially cut and shaped by man or been fortified by primitive stonework here and there; it seemed probable that the ruins we were seeking would be found somewhere in the body of this splendid bastion.

We descended the col, making our way painfully through intricate barriers of thorns which the natives living on the lower slopes had apparently constructed as baboon-traps. Why the baboons should go into them, as we did, instead of confining themselves to other parts of the hill, was not at first clear; but it transpired that the baboons lived chiefly in the higher rocks, and that the thorny maze was designed to discourage them from crossing the col and coming down to the mealie-fields that we had seen earlier. We certainly found, when we had crossed the valley and were climbing the steeper face, that we had come into baboon territory, for we surprised two troops of them within half a mile; they sprang away downhill to the ledges of a cliff, and followed our progress from a distance, barking indignantly.

The sun was now unbearably hot, filtering down in a chequered dazzle through the trees, which were too small to afford more than a momentary shade. The grass was less high, but the ground was strewn with boulders and dead thorns, and the grass itself concealed numerous ant-bear holes and fallen branches. The gradient had become increasingly steep; one had often to haul oneself up by handfuls of grass and we no longer spoke, having no breath to spare. I several times stumbled and fell, and could hear nothing but the noise of my own panting, which was too urgent to disguise. When we came to the crags at last and dragged ourselves up them there was nothing to do but sink on the warm rock, the blood roaring in our ears and all of us speechless.

When he had regained his breath, which he did with enviable ease, our elderly guide courteously beckoned us across the promontory on which we found ourselves and pointed to some clumps of grass and flowering aloe growing in fissures of the rock. We gazed at them blankly, and then saw, as he continued to beckon and point, that in the midst of this tangle of growth and partly concealed was another concrete survey-mark, rather bigger than Lusongo's, with a capital 'M' on one side of it, and a capital 'R' on the other. This, then, was the official summit of M'jenami, and marked the exact boundary between Mozambique and Rhodesia. We nodded and were turning away, more interested in our first view of the seemingly empty plains of Mozambique, when our guide electrified us by saying to Michael that this was the ruin we had wished to see, and that he was happy to have been able to bring us to it.

He seemed sad but not surprised when told that it was nothing of the sort, and that he must take Shorty and the two recruits and search the summit until they found some traces of ancient stonework. He withdrew meekly with the others behind a rock, where they held a whispered conference, and then squatted on their heels at a little distance and did nothing. It was very puzzling, but we did not greatly care, for though Michael was concerned for our disappointment and eager to resume the search as soon as we were rested, we had in fact found what we had come for, which was a view of the flat country of the M'rongwezi and a glimpse of farther hills as yet unnamed. The crag on which we stood jutted sharply out into the empty air, over a dizzy drop. Below that again the skirts of M'jenami spread steeply down and away to an endless plain, dotted with trees and clothed in yellow grass. We could see for many miles into Mozambique, but though we raked the plain with field-glasses there was no sign of any trail or habitation. Only, at about five or seven miles' distance, there was a serpentine line of denser vegetation which could have been larger trees, and suggested the presence of a river. Peter and Jack took sights and calculated distances and decided that this meandering line was the M'rongwezi. Its course was discernible for a considerable distance, being lost at length in a shimmer of light and heat which veiled it like a haze. In rainy weather visibility would have been greater, but there had not been a wisp of cloud for many days, and even the outlines of M'jenami quivered. We could not tell whether it would be possible to reach the river by Land Rover, or to follow its course when we got there. We had reached a country in which the only sure way of travelling was on foot.

To the north-east, where Russell's map had led us to expect it, we could see the bluish outline of rising hills. How far they extended, or what their height might be, there was no telling; but there was one neatly rounded summit, almost the shape of an ant-hill, which caught our attention. It was not marked on our maps and our guide and his aides could not identify it, never having been over the border into 'Portuguese'. Peter took careful sights and made a tentative pencil mark on the map. If we could positively identify any of these features we would be able to calculate our next move, and with luck might strike Umgila's kraal, where we hoped it would not be remembered how recklessly Russell and his friends had hanged the headman.

We reckoned that from the western foot of M'jenami, where we had started, to this eastern summit was roughly seven miles. There was nothing to be done now but go down again, for the descent could hardly take less than a couple of hours, and there would be only a narrow margin of daylight left. There was no time to look farther for ruins even if we wished to; in any case it had become obvious that so long as we stayed with our present guide we should find nothing. From his general demeanour and that of his supporters, as well as from various grins and winks from Shorty, we suspected that he had never had the smallest knowledge of any ruins, while the other two might possibly know the place but were not going to show it. The trip had been worth their while for the few shillings, and the Europeans had been gulled into the bargain. Our best plan, after all, would be to waste no more time on local talent but go straight to the chief Zamchiya, who was a mission-educated man and therefore, one would guess, less likely to be ruled by superstition. We did not know how far his territory extended but we knew it went some way into Mozambique and so must certainly include M'jenami. If he himself would give us a guide we should have an excuse for trying the mountain again, and might even (this was the point) gain information about the river and some of the hills beyond it.

We made our way down in a thoughtful silence broken only by occasional rifle-shots from Michael, who was relieving his feelings by shooting at several baboons. When the time came for our extra guides to leave us they cheered up noticeably, and the elder of the two, who kept a large drum hanging from one of the posts of his hut, regaled us with a farewell tattoo. We were gravely joined during this performance by the headman of the place, a frail-looking ancient with the pierced ears of a Zulu, dressed in a straight cotton skirt and a very old, shrunken and dust-coloured cardigan. He courteously insisted on walking back with us to the Land Rover, but when we apologized for having no present to offer him (a customary gesture of politeness from passing strangers) he accepted a two-shilling piece with dignity and went his way.

The only other being whom we saw as we came down the lower slopes was a nearly naked white boy herding goats, from whom our guide and Shorty averted their eyes as from an evil omen. He did not see us at first, being absorbed in urinating among his flock, his back towards us and his head bent; but so startling an apparition brought us to a standstill. His skin was as light as ours and his close-cropped cap of hair perfectly white; as he peered from side to side we saw that his eyes were screwed up and his face distorted with the effort of contending against the light. He was, in fact, an albino. These freaks, Michael told us, were not uncommon, for he had seen a good many in his lifetime here and there. They were tolerated, though regarded as a misfortune. This tolerance struck us as strange in people who regarded any abnormality as evil, who smother first-born twins as the work of devils and meet a difficult labour with punishment as proof of adultery; the missionaries were finding it uphill work to discourage such practices. Yet the albino was reluctantly accepted, though no one cared to encounter one. For Shorty and our guide the poor white boy was a dubious portent for the day of our first attempt on M'jenami.

Before having another try at the mountain there was much to be done if we did not wish to repeat the first day's failure. We must ask help from Zamchiya, for our experience with guides so far had convinced us that any we were likely to find for ourselves would be useless. Either they would know nothing and would not say so, or they would go to elaborate lengths to confuse and mislead us. Anything not understood must be kept hidden; a curse might fall on the man who showed the haunts of the dead to curious strangers. Russell, we remembered, had thought it possible that a mission-convert—'one of these educated gentlemen' as he slightingly put it—might be willing to reveal Umgila's grave for money. We had not got so far as that yet, and were not going to mention Umgila until we had to, since the name itself was dangerous; but we felt that Zamchiya, being a man of some education and used to the eccentricities of Europeans, might be willing to give us a guide and some sensible information about the country.

Before we could approach him, however, the Land Rover needed skilled attention. The steering was growing worse and Peter spent his spare time under the chassis, tinkering crossly with wholly inadequate tools and thinking of all the things that could happen as a result of the damage. I think it was at this point that Michael began to get seriously on his nerves, and a tension built up which was nourished by trivial incidents. Michael was optimistic and happy-go-lucky; according to him, one bashed through problems somehow; it would be all right on the night. Peter was cautious and exact; he saw no reason to suppose that a damaged mechanism would not give way when it was least convenient, and was irritated by cheerful assertions that we could fake up a spare somehow when we had neither the skill nor the equipment. He became acidly polite to Michael over the tools, which Michael constantly borrowed for the lorry and lost in the grass; and after a time the politeness wore thin and did not cover the acidity. Peter and Michael were both great borrowers, and soon we were all (with the exception of Michael, who had nothing to lend) involved in a crafty game of concealing essential equipment from one another. Electric torches, soap, toilet paper, matches, the kettle were always disappearing out of one's tent and if we made a truce on these things with one another we lost them to the cook, who had always mislaid everything belonging to the kitchen and came prowling round after sunset like a jackal. This is one of the phases, I believe, through which all expeditions pass, and which old campaigners learn to survive with good temper. We, being novices, were in the learning stage, and had often cause to be thankful that Jack was born to be a peacemaker. The *munts*, incidentally, saw more of this than we supposed, for being unable to grasp our real names they referred to us always by native ones descriptive of behaviour. Michael, whom they knew, was 'Boss Michael', but I was 'The-woman-who-loves-the-fire', and Jack (apt description) 'He-who-desires-peace'. Peter I am sorry to say, being named in a difficult period, was 'He-who-is-often-in-a-rage'; but this we thought it politic not to communicate.

Rightly obsessed by the Land Rover's symptoms, and alarmed to find that the drums of petrol and diesel oil which we carried in the lorry were unaccountably low, Peter decided that there was nothing to do but return to Chipinga for repairs and supplies before we went farther. He cringed with apprehension whenever Michael went off for wood or water in the Land Rover, driving with fearless dash as though on an assault course; sooner or later, he knew, something would give, and land us in some unspeakable predicament. Michael was also fretting to move camp, for all the old reasons which had to do with rivers, and accordingly once more we planned to separate. After much studying of maps and some mutually irritating argument a meeting-place was fixed at a drift across the Umzilizwe River, which we privately reckoned would bring us within reasonable distance of Zamchiya's village, also of a point at which we might cross the border into Mozambique. We would meet there in three days' time and look for a new camp.

When we passed through Chikore we paused only long enough to confirm our guess that the mission had no repair-shop, and to accept with gratitude the offer of a night's stay on our return. It was extraordinary to discover what a changed aspect Chipinga now wore when we came into it after ten days in the bush. Before, it had seemed the final depressing remnant of everything most distasteful in 'civilization'. Now it was a metropolis, and we found ourselves gazing at its dead-end street and shoddy buildings with something like excitement. It was like home to join the queue in the one-room bank, open for its weekly three-hour session, and see the teller at work with a half-eaten apple and a revolver beside the till. The Italian hotel proprietor was an old friend, glad to see us in the bar since business was poor owing to the influence of the Dutch Reformed Church —'but they drink plenty brandy at home, is bad for business'. Meikles' store and the Greek bazaar in the back street were dazzling in the variety of their goods, and we spent a happy hour shopping for water-bags and torch batteries. Best of all was to soak in a hot bath at the hotel and have our clothes washed, for the soil of the Chimedzi camp had been composed of reddish dust so fine that it rose in a cloud whenever one moved, sifting into hair, clothes, everything. Nor was this all, for it was the evening of the 'Free Bioscope Show' which is the peak of Chipinga's social entertainment, and we gaped through several hours of motor-oil and farming documentaries, sitting on hard chairs with our mouths open.

After twenty-four hours of these pleasures the Land Rover was ready, the fuel drums loaded and luxuries like fresh bread and vegetables packed around our feet. The steering felt healthy again and we reached Chikore without mishap in the evening, rehearsing a number of questions to which we hoped to get answers from the missionaries. These were chiefly to do with place-names, for the time had come when we felt we must get some clue to Russell's likeliest route from the M'rongwezi and to the identity of the hill called Kyabanga. Unfortunately Mr Blakney was away for that night, and no one felt able to advise on points which depended on differences between Chindau and Zulu. He was expected back some time the following day, and in the meantime they would give us guides to some known Bantu ruins which could be seen about seven miles away from the mission.

This was a loss of time, but it could not be helped. Once we had left Chikore we might never be able openly to ask questions, and trivial though they might seem to the uninitiated, to us they were important. The nearer we came to it, the more dangerous it might be to mention Kyabanga; the ideal would be to gather some private knowledge by chance. So we displayed a proper enthusiasm for the ruins, since we were determined if possible to wait for Mr Blakney, and were sent off with two youths from the secondary school called Robert and Adonis. Robert, the younger, had been chosen because he positively knew the ruins; Adonis because he spoke English and had brains. It is difficult to judge the age of Africans, but I imagine they were about fifteen and seventeen. The missionaries had been amused and sympathetic over our failure on M'jenami, and assured us that these boys, being Christians, would be unlikely to mislead us through superstition. And so indeed it proved. After some miles of the usual intolerable trail, winding always steeply uphill into a cooler air and an almost English type of vegetation, they led us through a rank-smelling thicket and parted the leaves to show us the crumbling remains of stone walls. Nothing was left of them now but their foundations, about four feet thick and two or three feet high. They were dry-stone walls, carefully built of uncut slabs, such as one sees in Gloucestershire, and so hidden and overgrown with trees and brambles that it was impossible to form any accurate idea of the shape of the original structure, though we guessed it to be roughly in the form of a ring, and the diameter, which we paced, was over three hundred feet. It had been built on the very crown of the hill and ran right to the edge of an escarpment, looking over a splendid gorge and endless empty miles of forest and bush. Robert, the younger boy, had become uneasy as soon as we came into this place, but Adonis was more sophisticated and scrambled about with us, peering under the leaves. When I asked him, however, to cut away a stout ivy with his *panga* so that I could take a photograph, the amiable smile faded from his face and he said in a shocked voice, 'The trees must not be cut.'

When we got back to Chikore, Mr Blakney had not returned. We lingered uneasily, afraid of outstaying our welcome in this busy place, where everyone, husbands and wives alike, seemed to rush from classroom to classroom all day long and there was no end to the orderly bell-ringing and chanting; but we wished, we said, to say good-bye to him, and packed our things in the Land Rover very slowly. And at last, just as we were shaking hands with our kind hosts, another Land Rover bumped across the campus and an energetic figure dived towards the white-washed bungalow which served as an office. We caught him on the steps, and in the midst of much jovial hand-shaking I drew him aside and showed him a paper on which I had written some names, asking for help on spelling and pronunciation. Yes, he said after a moment, Umgila and Umzila were the same. He had heard of him; he had been a chief, he thought, some place or other; since it was a Zulu name Umzila would certainly be the correct version. He had never heard of Mandhlami or his kraal, and shook his head dubiously over Kyabanga. Was it the name of a person or a place? What had my uncle said about it? There was a word in Chindau, *kabanga*, which meant 'perhaps': could this have any bearing on the matter? I did not like the sound of it at all, for it seemed suddenly and dreadfully possible that this might have been, indeed, what Russell had heard; though on second thoughts his fair knowledge of the language made it improbable. 'See here, though,' said Mr Blakney, frown-ing at the paper, 'come and see Fred Sigauke in the office. He's our primary out-schools clerk and language expert, he taught us all what little Chindau we know.'

He took us into a bare room where Mrs Abbott and one or two young and serious-looking Africans were unpacking crates of school-books and stacking them on shelves. With them was a middle-aged, stout, extremely black man whose face creased into a smile at the sight of strangers and who was introduced to us as Mr Sigauke. Yes, he knew the border country all right. Yes, yes, there was a kraal called Mandhlaame; he pronounced it Mandla-ame, and corrected the spelling on my paper, holding it against a text-book close to his face. Peter and Jack affected to examine bookshelves, unable to bear the suspense of the next question. Did he happen to know a hill called Kyabanga? The office was suddenly quiet; I held my breath. Mr Sigauke burst into a jolly laugh. Well, yes, he knew the hill, but I pronounced it wrong. It was *Nyabánga*, and it meant something, yes, yes, let him think, it meant 'he who flourishes the big knife'. Did he know by any chance where the hill was? We had heard the name, and thought we would like to see it. Oh yes, he knew it very well. He had never been there, but he knew it was over the border in Mozambique. As casually as I could, I unfolded our best, but now tattered and dust-stained map. Could he show us the place perhaps? There was always a chance that we might be going that way. He put on his spectacles and moved his finger doubtfully over the map. Well, here perhaps, or here; he could not say exactly. I saw that his finger was wandering lost in the middle of Southern Rhodesia, and that the map meant nothing to him, and was a mystery. It was all bush, he said. Very sorry. He could not precisely tell.

This was enough, however, to send us off from Chikore privately rejoicing. There could be no doubt now about the name of the hill. Or could there? We made valiant attempts to distrust our swelling optimism, to maintain that the difference of a letter must not be ignored, that the hill was not necessarily our hill because all the other details fell into place. It was no use. The river was similar in name and identical in position with the one on Russell's map. 'Mandhlami's kraal' was certainly Mandhla-ame, since it was customary for a kraal to bear the name of its chief, as Zamchiya stood both for the place and the man. The hills we had seen were where Russell had marked the fringe of the high veldt; and now the word which we had carried from the beginning as a talisman had been recognized and confirmed as the name of a hill some miles into Mozambique, in the direction in which we had always believed we should find it. If only the hill could be identified from a distance we should be spared the doubtful search for Umzila's kraal, which now, more than forty

years since Russell had dug his trenches, might well be un-
identifiable. If Zamchiya could give us a guide who could do
this for us we should go straight to the spot on which our
search depended, without losing time in a hunt for obliterated
villages.

Michael was found at the drift, according to plan, not at all
discouraged by the long hours of waiting and passing the time
with Shorty in washing the lorry. This river was a tributary
of the Umzilizwe and still had water in it, which encouraged us
to follow a trail to the north-east, where we expected to strike
the Umzilizwe proper. This trail was by far the worst we had
yet struck; the vehicles groaned and crashed from rock to rock,
and as mile succeeded mile we were dismayed to think how often
they would have to tackle it, since there would be no other way of
leaving or returning to camp. But the Umzilizwe itself seemed
almost worth it. It was a real river even at this season, running
through a succession of wooded gorges above the spot we finally
decided on, where it spread itself into shallows that could be
crossed on foot. Here the ground was level and the air sweet.
Wooded hills rose up on either side and there was ample shade.
The tents were pitched within a few yards of the river and our
chairs set out in a little bower of trees which the sun could not
penetrate even at midday. As usual we were farther off than we
wished to be, in the *cul-de-sac* of a rough and destructive trail,
but we had learned to be thankful for peace and running water,
and in this bosky place even the *munts* seemed happy. In no
time at all John had got the bushes full of washing, the cook was
squatting in the shallows scouring saucepans, and Shorty,
watched by some giggling girls on the farther bank, was taking a
modest bath in the river with his clothes on.

We decided to rest for at least a day in camp, since Jack was
still troubled with sore throat and a general feeling of lassitude
and malaise, and was trying all the pills in the medical bag with
discouraging results. The river itself was tempting to explore,

and after a peaceful night we made our way on foot through the gorges to some hidden falls, and passed the day in the roar and spray of their waters. After so many days in the burnt-up bush this green and virgin place was an oasis. It was so hidden under rose-red cliffs and hanging forest that one could easily believe no human being had ever been there before, and indeed during the whole of that halcyon day we saw no one. The invisible deity of the pool was presumably a crocodile, whose basking place Michael found on a well-worn ledge, where the grass was littered with stinking fish-bone fragments, and there was a convenient muddy slide into the river. This made Michael, for one, deeply happy, for he was ashamed of having never shot a crocodile, and carried a paper-back treatise on the subject wherever he went. He was intent all day on luring the creature into view, but it knew a trick worth two of that and remained submerged, while Michael fretted along the bank with his gun, eyeing every floating twig and fragment of bark in the hope that they might turn out to be crocodiles' nostrils. Shadow was eventually sent into the pool, being an old campaigner who had done battle with a crocodile in his time, and when even this living bait failed Michael himself went in, looking deliciously edible and gingerly swimming about with a hunting-knife. He took the precaution of getting Jack to stand on the bank with a rifle, but how this would help, if the crocodile should decide to engage, was never made clear. I think Jack was relieved at not having to distinguish between them in a hurry.

The next morning, while Peter and Michael explored some disorder of the lorry, which was refusing to start unless towed for a short distance by the Land Rover, Jack and I set out to find Zamchiya. Our best approach to the chief was through Mr Hla-Hla, whose farm and store we knew, and who was reputed to be an enterprising character. We found him to be both intelligent and charming, with a fair command of English and eager to talk. He was so civil and communicative indeed, and so evidently flattered at being consulted about anything so educational as ruins, that we were devoutly thankful not to have Michael with us. One curt demand, one thoughtless touch of lordly Rhodesian manner, and Mr Hla-Hla, we guessed, would have been lost to us. He had been schooled himself at Mount Selinda and was clearly one of those forward-looking Africans who are more than half in love with the white man's world. He asked at once if we came from a university, concealing his disappointment when he heard that we had only an amateur's interest in archæology. Were there really ruins on M'jenami, he asked? He had never heard of them, but then Africa was littered with ancient ruins which white Rhodesians insisted were not Bantu. They had to be the work of the Portuguese, or of Arab traders—anything rather than admit that the African might have been clever enough to build them. Chief Zamchiya might know something, certainly; he, Joel Hla-Hla, would take us at once to the school and introduce us.

Zamchiya school was larger and tidier than Mariya; it even had flower-beds of a sort, which we pretended to study while Hla-Hla, hat in hand, went the round of the classrooms looking for the Chief. When Zamchiya at last emerged, he looked so genuine that our hearts failed us. He was a tall, powerful-looking man of perhaps fifty-five, dressed as we were in crumpled khaki cotton, but with a dignity of demeanour that was impressive; there was no mistaking that air of ancient authority. We exchanged courtesies, everything having become suddenly formal. We could not tell from his face, which was impassive, nor from Hla-Hla's, which was anxious, whether or not the Chief were pleased to see us. Our intrusion in the middle of school was perhaps an impertinence, for all that he said when he had read the letter was, 'I see.' His reserved manner, however, meant nothing unfavourable, and was more probably due to the surprise of the occasion. M'jenami, he said, was in his territory, and when we made our request for a guide he considered a little, and eventually said he would take us there himself.

This was better than we had hoped for, and we went back to

camp in a state of nervous elation. Zamchiya, being Chief of the district, would know the country; as an educated man and a Christian he would probably have no objection to showing us anything; but he might also—and this was a thought which gave us pause—know all about Umzila and his treasure, and be suspicious of Europeans in his territory. Was it this, perhaps, that had made him decide to accompany us himself? Or was his offer simply a gentlemanly gesture? One thing was certain: we must keep Michael as much as possible out of his company, since any brusqueness or ordering about would be fatal, and our hopes would depend entirely on good relations.

We held a furtive conference with Peter, and decided that the best thing would be to persuade Michael to go off by himself for a couple of days to shoot, while we concentrated on the Chief and M'jenami. Fortunately he needed no persuading; he had been disgusted all along by the scarcity of game, and the thought of the tsetse-fly man at Hippo Mine, happily shooting everything in sight, continually fretted him. He jumped at the idea, eagerly agreeing that ruins were not in his line and that it would be better for him to bring back some buck for the larder. He would go off in the morning in the lorry, taking John; the cook and Shorty would feed us and look after the camp, and Shadow would stay and afford us his protection. It wouldn't do, he said as a simple pleasantry, to come back and find we had all been eaten by leopards. 'Though as a matter of fact,' he added reassuringly, 'a leopard rarely attacks a human being. They'll always take a *munt* by preference, if there's a choice.'

Next morning we rose in the dark and breakfasted at sunrise, while Michael prepared the lorry for Hippo Mine. Jack was feeling worse; he complained of headache and was quite voiceless, and had also a slight temperature, so it seemed sensible that he should stay in camp. Shadow, too, had plans of his own, for when he had received his orders and the lorry started he shot like a missile after it and was not seen again. Listening, we heard the lorry stop and start again, and guessed that Shadow had gained his point and would now be sitting erect in the passenger seat, willingly enduring Michael's half-hearted scolding.

Peter and I set off in the Land Rover, bracing ourselves for the first five miles of the trail, which we had named Dead Man's Gulch and which was as murderous as ever. It seemed only a matter of time before the Land Rover would be literally shaken to pieces. By contrast the trails on the other side of the drift seemed almost like roads, and we sighed with relief as we rattled and bumped along them to Zamchiya.

The Chief emerged from the school as soon as we arrived, beautifully dressed for the expedition in starched and well-pressed khaki jacket and shorts, dazzlingly polished boots, a felt hat with a leopard-skin hat-band, and his brass badge of chiefly office gleaming on a chain at his breast. He seemed pleased at the prospect of a day off, and carried a basket of oranges.

We left the Land Rover at the 'baboon village' as before, and here the Chief surprised us by recommending, as our first guide had done, that we should climb Lusongo instead. This shook our confidence for the moment, for we thought we had already passed that tiresome phase; but he agreed amiably enough to M'jenami and led us briskly into the high grass, forging uphill at a good four miles an hour. The route he chose was more circuitous than our first, and led steadily round to the other side of the mountain. Our hopes began to revive, for he walked with the purposeful speed of a man who knows where he is going and is oblivious of lesser beings panting behind him. We did not pant so much in the first two hours while he kept to the lower slopes, passing through a number of scattered smallholdings, but when once he began to climb it was cruel work, and no matter how harsh the ascent, through rocks and thorns and tangled nets of creeper, it seemed to me that his speed never slackened. I struggled a long way below the others, with crazed thoughts of burst lungs and heart-failure, and not enough breath to shout after them for a halt. My boots were beginning to give trouble, for having been bought in Salisbury, where apparently boots for women are unknown, they were two sizes too big, and in spite of two pairs of socks were slipping abominably. I could feel the blisters rising on my heels, and as the skin of my toes wore through I thought almost with tears of the beautiful hand-made boots which anyone with a grain of sense would have had made in London. I had to stop at last, for the corrosive ridges in my socks were beyond bearing, and when finally my non-appearance was noticed Zamchiya came nimbly back to see what had happened, and stood over me, not out of breath at all but gently concerned, and peeled me one of his beautiful quenching oranges.

At the end of the last and worst ascent, scrambling in painful silence up ledges and crags, it was a shock to find ourselves on the very spot that we had reached on our first climb. Here were the clump of aloes, the survey mark, the blackened ashes of our fire. Peter and I sat down in silence under a rock. Presently Zamchiya collected and kindled some sticks, and when we had breath we questioned him. It now transpired that he had never heard of any ruins, and thought it was the summit crags we had wished to see. Whether he had really understood us I have no idea, but he being the man he was (if one can ever judge any-body) we believed he was speaking the truth. It did not greatly matter. We were gazing over the plains of his Portuguese terri-tory, with the shadowy thread of the river distantly visible and the blue-smudged hills far off on the eastern horizon. These were what we had wished to see in his company, and when we had shared our coffee and bully-beef I took some photographs of the view as a preliminary to asking some innocent questions.

Did M'jenami, the name of the mountain, mean anything? 'Oh yes,' he said, 'there is a meaning. It means . . . now let me see . . . "the rocks that laugh".' We pondered this for a while, not liking it much. There was, he went on, hesitating for words, a belief among his people that a great lion inhabited these rocks, and that was perhaps what made our guides unwilling. They were, of course, he said deprecatingly, superstitious. They had strong feelings against showing anything to white men, since everything ancient belonged to spirits, even these rocks, and they were afraid of what might happen if things were disturbed. Europeans were apt to disturb by digging. This was well known. They were always looking for gold and precious stones, and the people believed, if such things had ever been buried in the earth, that they had been put there for good reason, and must remain hidden. He shook his head indulgently over this idea, while Peter and I stared at him in fascination, searching for hidden meaning in his expression. We found none. That was why, he continued, he had thought it best to show us the mountain himself. He understood, if he did not share, these feelings, and would be sorry to see us misled.

A little shaken by this conversation, and silently wondering how many of the Chief's people remembered Russell, who had passed that way and hanged a headman while Zamchiya was a boy, we moved to the edge of the rocks and asked him to show us the limits of his territory. He considered a little, shading his eyes with his hand, then pointed to the tree-lined curve of the M'rongwezi. 'As far as the river,' he said, 'if you can see it. I end there.' And in the other direction, I asked, how far did he go? He shifted his ground and pointed to the north-east. 'I go to that hill.'

'That mound-shaped one, do you mean? Like an ant-heap?'

'Yes, that one.'

'What is the name of that hill?'

'It is called Guma.'

I had a sensation as though my heart had dropped, and knew what extravagant hopes had hung on his answer. There was a silence, and we all gazed at the hill.

'Is that the native name?'

'Oh no, it is Portuguese. We call it differently.'

'What is the native name?'

'It is Nyabánga.'

We slowly took out our field-glasses, praising the view. Peter and I did not look at one another. Seen through the glass it was quite a sizeable hill, symmetrical and without any noticeable feature beyond a large tree distinguishable near the summit. We turned away after a brief look, nervous as to how the conversation might develop; but Zamchiya had already gone back to the fire and was stamping it out methodically with his boot. He seemed mildly worried still that we had found no ruins, and suggested that we should go down by a different way. This meant a long and agonizing detour, in which eventually nothing to me seemed desirable but to fall with a cry on the ground and give up the struggle. Down we stumbled through rocks and thorns and the abominable grass, which concealed endless pitfalls and closed at times triumphantly over my head. I seemed to float at last through a trance of fatigue, my body falling forward as though through deep water and my limbs propelled by a power outside myself. There were light-headed moments when I told myself, and believed, that an influence sustained me which came from Nyabánga.

7

The Approach to Nyabánga

THE camp was very quiet without Michael. The cook and Shorty were on their best behaviour, nobody whistled or sang or did target practice, Jack was better, and after M'jenami it was wonderful to spend the next day doing nothing. I washed my hair and read *Edwin Drood* while Peter fished peacefully for barbel. With Shadow away the birds were noticeably bolder, and a small donkey which seemed to belong to nobody had wandered up from the river and was grazing along the sweet grass of the bank. I had been a little dubious about sleeping out by myself, since my bed was a good way off from the tents and the nights were dark; but everything had been quiet and re-assuring and I had slept the sleep of exhaustion beside the fire.

On the second night, though, I was startled broad awake about midnight by a stealthy sound which my ears interpreted as someone tripping over the washing-up bowl. This large enamel object was always to be found lying somewhere in the grass, surrounded by sundry bits of the cook's equipment, and the sound of its being shifted was unmistakable. My first thought, as I sat up in bed with a start, was that Shorty and the cook must have sneaked off to a beer-drinking without per-mission, and had stumbled tipsily over the thing in the dark. After a time, however, as there was no further sound, I concluded that they had found their way to bed, and lay down again. Just as my muscles had relaxed and I had begun to drowse, the noise was repeated. This time there was no mistaking it. The big bowl had been pushed aside by something, and had touched another object with a light clank. I raised myself cautiously on one elbow and played the beam of my torch over the camp. The battery was a new one and the beam strong, but it showed nothing. No one was stirring: the camp was as still as death. The fire had died down completely, and after listening uneasily to the silence I got out of bed and tried to coax a flame out of the ashes. It revived soon enough, for the trench was still red-hot under the surface and I built it up with wood to a bright blaze. Now I could see more clearly, and assured myself that there was nothing there. The *munts* had not stirred from their tarpaulin and bushes and grass were motionless. I got back into bed and lay awake for a while, hearing a stealthy sound from time to time as though something were nosing about among empty tins, but I was convinced by now that it could be nothing more than one of the skin-and-bone kaffir dogs that we sometimes saw, taking advantage of Shadow's absence to do a little opportune scavenging.

In the morning, making his way through the bushes behind the camp, Peter stumbled over the front half of the donkey, lying clotted with blood and almost hidden in the grass. The hind-quarters and legs had been eaten completely; even the bones were gone; the ribs stuck out from tatters of hide and flesh. We stood round the sorry spectacle in amazement. From the look of the grass it was evident that the body had been somehow dragged through the camp, disturbing the cook's muddles in its passage, and been taken to this discreet spot to be devoured. It seemed extraordinary that dogs, however hungry, could accomplish such a thing, and we were mystified afresh when as the morning wore on they began to appear in timid ones and twos, skirting nervously round the bushes and appearing almost too frightened to approach their meal. How had these small and skinny creatures killed it? They made progress with the carcase during the day, but far less than they had managed during the night, and the head, shoulders and forelegs remained uneaten. The dogs disappeared at sundown, and the third night was quiet and without incident.

We had been expecting Michael all that day, but he had not returned, and we were wondering how long we should wait before crossing the border into Mozambique. Zamchiya had offered to show us the way when we were ready, and we were glad of this, being anxious not to do anything which might attract attention from the Portuguese. The nearest Portuguese Native Commissioner was at Spungabera, about thirty miles away as the crow flies, but news travels mysteriously in the bush, and a party of Europeans crossing the border without permission was likely to be reported soon enough. If Zamchiya went with us he would not only show us the way, but by his presence allay suspicion in his own people. If he allowed us to camp in his Portuguese territory we should be accepted; if not, we judged it would not be many days before the news of our presence reached Spungabera.

The pleasurable suspense of being at last within reach of Nyabánga was beginning to throw up sideshoots of uneasiness which I did not altogether like. I did not like the idea of the

Portuguese, whose native administration was known to be severe. They might be unpleasantly interested in treasure, and would take a harsh view of foreigners looking for it. Nor did I care for the notion—indeed the more I thought of it the less I liked it—of accepting Zamchiya's help in an enterprise which, if he understood it at all, would certainly appal him. He had impressed us all as a man of unusual quality, whom it was hateful to deceive; but of course we really knew nothing, it was equally possible that he had suspected us from the start, and was going with us for his own precautionary ends. We even canvassed the idea, sitting round the fire on this last night, that it might be prudent to take him into our confidence; but such recklessness was out of the question. What would Russell have said to such pusillanimous behaviour? We needed the moral stiffening of Michael's presence if we were not to be corrupted by feelings of guilty sympathy towards Africans, and his absence underlined yet another uncomfortable thought—that Michael, sooner or later, would have to be told.

He returned about three o'clock the next morning, crashing into camp in a blaze of headlights, with noise and shouting that brought us tumbling from our beds. He was so late because he had had a puncture twelve miles after leaving Hippo Mine, and having naturally forgotten to take a spanner, had had to walk that distance back to borrow one. He reported the area as being seething with game, as he had expected; he had even found hippo spoor round his bed that morning. He had shot a couple of buck and was feeling much happier. He was grimy and tired and had grown the beginnings of a beard, which he had decided not to shave off since it was his first, and an object of great interest.

Even the beard was forgotten, however, when he was searching about the bushes for something he had lost, and stumbled over the poor remains of our donkey. This was a lion kill, he said; how on earth had we managed not to know anything about it? We stood round the sorry fragments once more and I told him about the disturbances of the night and the kaffir dogs which

I thought might be responsible; but he insisted that this was the work of a young lion. Dogs could not possibly have done it, and a leopard, according to custom, would have left the uneaten half of the corpse in a tree, where it would be safe from scavengers. He was amused to think that I had been getting in and out of bed and mending the fire while the lion was patiently waiting in the grass, and said that it could never have happened if Shadow had been there. This was probably true, and I was glad that it was the donkey and not I that had been pulled into the bushes in his absence. In retrospect, the night had concealed a number of possibilities.

When we had all digested the subject and Michael had been fed, he hung up the buck by the heels in a tree and fell asleep by the fire, not waking even when his blankets began to smoulder and I was jerked out of strange dreams by the smell of burning. He slept so late the following day that we had to give up the idea of moving camp, and the afternoon was spent on the theory and practice of making biltong. This was a serious performance, and though I shall probably never need to do it again I like to remember how Michael made it, and the gravity with which he performed the ritual.

First, he said, one cut strips of buttock meat, an inch thick and about two inches wide, and slopped it around in a cupful of warm water with three teaspoonsfuls of pepper. It was soaked and moved around for about an hour. Then it was taken out, squeezed, and soaked for an hour or two in warm salt water. It was then dried, a handful of coarse salt was put in a basin, the meat dipped in this and the salt well rubbed in. (This salting and peppering, he explained, was both to preserve the meat and keep the flies off it.) Finally it was hung in a tree in the shade for several days, until it was hard and dry. When it was black outside and nearly dry through it would be ready. The whole thing took hours and looked nasty, but Michael was pleased, and when we moved camp next morning the biltong was carefully unhooked and travelled with us.

We moved in slow convoy, Jack and Zamchiya and I ahead in the Land Rover, Michael and Peter, Shadow, the *munts* and everything else piled high in the lorry. (I had asked Michael, as a concession to me and my funny ideas, to be specially nice to Zamchiya, Hla-Hla and any other Africans to whom we felt friendly: he had promised, in a teasing fashion, but we did not wish to try him too sorely by putting them cheek by jowl.) The Chief had been collected from his house early in the morning, and had loaded us with splendid presents of eggs and fruit. A basket as big as a cradle had been filled with oranges of that delicious and tangerine-like sort called *naartjes*, and at the last moment he had cut two small pineapples from their prickly stalks, growing almost on the ground beside his garden path. As we drove, the lovely smell of all this fruit rose up from the littered floor of the Land Rover and was a pleasure in our nostrils.

After an hour of following a well-trodden track we were seven miles into Mozambique and at the limits of the Chief's territory. We emerged from the bush on to a bare open space, and saw that we were no more than a mile or two from Nyabánga. It rose up in a steep cone of grass and trees, without any sign of rocks or habitation. We could not judge the height of the grass, but from this distance it looked fairly easy to climb; the trees were the usual scrub growth, the only conspicuous feature being the one big tree near the summit, darker in colour than the rest, which we had seen from M'jenami. In the midst of the open ground, trodden hard by the feet of men and cattle, was a line of substantial open sheds with a corral at either end, which had clearly not been built by Africans. This was a cattle-dip, built on Portuguese territory by the Rhodesian Government, we were told, owing to a mistake over the exact position of the border. The sheds concealed a deep trough, filled with a grey and evil-smelling chemical which discouraged ticks; the cattle for miles around were driven through it once a week. On the far side of this open area was a line of trees with a few green banners of banana showing among them, and it was here that

Zamchiya recommended us to camp, as the trees concealed a drift across a river. This seemed too good to be true, as indeed it was, for the river proved to be no more than a pestilent-looking trickle where cattle and goats were watered and some women were washing rags in a muddy puddle. The drift was a busy highway, with a constant coming and going of women and children; the whole place was bare, sordid and public. When Michael arrived with the lorry he agreed at once that it was impossible to camp there; the water was dirty and insufficient and the place was totally lacking in shade and privacy. The only thing, it seemed, was to explore farther, following the trail along the river until we came to something better. Zamchiya was willing to go with us, but seemed very doubtful as to what we should find. The road was bad, he said; and this, coming from him, should have made us cautious, but we were anxious to make camp while daylight lasted, and impatient to get away from the distasteful place. We could see no harm in trying, and pushed on.

This was an atrocious mistake, as we soon discovered. The sensible course would have been to prospect ahead in the Land Rover, leaving the lorry at the dip; but this for some reason did not occur to us, and the two vehicles ground up a stony hill and dropped down into a narrow valley of dark rain-forest. Here the trail was narrow, hemmed in by boulders and trees on either side. The river had disappeared in a leafy chasm, and we climbed in and out of slippery gullies which in the rainy season must have been lively tributaries, but which now were precipitous troughs of stones and mud. There was no room to turn, so we could not go back, and whenever we paused in dismay at what lay ahead the heavy breathing of the diesel was close behind us. At length we were brought up short by a crash and a shout; the lorry had nose-dived into a narrow chine and was stuck in the bottom. The Land Rover had scrambled out with difficulty, but the lorry was too long for the width of the dip; it could not begin to climb from such an angle, with its hind wheels still so much higher than its head. There was nothing to do but unload it and let the Land Rover try to haul it out with chains, and this, after several discouraging attempts, succeeded, when we had cut armsfuls of branches for the wheels and paved the mud of the farther slope with stones. It came out at last with a huge roar of distress, and we tried not to think of the time when we should have to return.

With every mile that we covered our hearts sank, for though the river now had plenty of water in it and could be heard among the rocks some distance below, we were still held as in a vice in our narrow passage, hemmed in by steep banks of rocks and trees, with not an inch of level ground and no room to turn. When at last the trail dropped down to the level of the river and we began to hope, the trail itself broke out into such a nightmare stretch of rocks and boulders that Zamchiya and I dismounted in horror, leaving Jack to plunge and crash as best he could without having our extra weight in the suffering Land Rover. There were three of these stretches of hellish going, each lasting a quarter of a mile, and when they were passed the ground began to fall into gentler contours, and though the trail was still confined we moved easily. The road would soon, Zamchiya said, run into a big drift of the Umzilizwe, and this we should not be able to pass with safety. He would not be able to accompany us any farther, but thought that the place would make us a good camp. He had brought his bicycle in the back of the Land Rover, and on this he proposed to return to the cattle-dip, where there was a kraal which he was accustomed to visit regularly for the purpose of administering Chief Law. The only difficulty we had still to pass was a small bridge; it would bear our weight, he thought, though of course it had not been built for vehicles.

He had no sooner spoken than we came to it, and got out to have a look at this last hazard. It was a flimsy-looking construction of tree-trunks and branches, laid across the last of the narrow gullies that bedevilled the trail. Three sizeable tree-trunks had been laid across from side to side, and across these

again, lashed into place with creeper, was a thick uneven floor-
ing of stout branches. It did not look promising, but the gully
was deep, and there seemed no possible way of going round.
We unloaded the heaviest gear, and Peter, who had come up in
the lorry and was in a state of loving anxiety over the Land
Rover, took her over at a snail's pace while the rest of us stood by
helplessly, holding our breath. The timber sagged and creaked
but nothing broke, and we had now only to repeat the performance with the lorry. This, too, was unloaded, while Michael
looked at the bridge and decided his strategy. We had run a
great risk, he said, in taking the Land Rover slowly; if the bridge
had given in the middle we should never have got out. The
proper way was to take it at speed, so that the bridge hardly had
time to feel the weight. Adopting this method one could get over
practically anything, even with a four-ton lorry.

He reversed the lorry out of its litter of packing-cases and
had the road cleared. The diesel motor was roared to a deafening
pitch, backed a little farther, roared again, and then we were all
scattered in the grass by the lorry's charge. It went over with a
sickening bound, landing triumphantly as the bridge exploded
behind it in a shower of timber.

It needed only this to drive home to us the folly of not
leaving the lorry behind while we reconnoitred. We had now
arrived at a place where we could reasonably camp, but we were
six miles farther away from Nyabánga, cut off from the trail by a
broken bridge and more than three-quarters of a mile of murderous rocks. Peter went off at once to look at the bridge and
was away a long time; when he came back he announced that
there was a possible by-pass for the Land Rover, cutting through
the bush and taking the gully at a less precipitous point, but he
doubted it being practicable for the lorry. He was wearing his
most thunderous aspect, as though he did not greatly care if
Michael and the lorry were immobilized for good. Michael,
however, was as happy as a bird, having within five minutes of
arriving at this new river seen a seven-foot crocodile with his

own eyes; he was now plunging noisily about in the reeds, devising cunning plans for outwitting the monster.

The river was not in fact a new one, but our old acquaintance the Umzilizwe, flowing fast and strong. The bank on our side was extremely steep, a bare slope at a gradient of one in four. At the foot of this the river had been roughly dammed with stones and spread out to a width of forty or fifty yards; it was not more than knee-deep but the current was strong, pouring through the gaps in the dam into a flurry of broken water. The ground on the far side was level and easy, and the trail wound away into the farther hills, but we could see at once that it would be madness to try and take the vehicles across. Even if the water were not too deep the bed of the river was full of slippery boulders, and the deeper pools on our side and the steepness of the bank made it doubtful if we should be able to return. Fortunately there was no need to cross; we were already uncomfortably far from Nyabánga, and had no wish to go farther. We were now, Zamchiya said, in the territory of a chief he did not know, whose village was a day's march farther on and who spoke a different language. We would do better to stay on this side in any case, for the trail eventually led to Spungabera, and whoever followed it would sooner or later encounter the Portuguese.

We thanked him and said we would eventually return the way we had come, and would hope to see him again to say good-bye. For the present we would camp on this excellent river, to rest a while and take photographs of the country. We parted with mutual courtesies, and on our part a real unwillingness to see him go. He had proved himself so far a kindly friend, and his smiling face and gentle bearing rebuked any lingering thoughts of past suspicion. He mounted his bicycle and wobbled off, a dignified and sympathetic figure.

The new camp occupied our thoughts and energies for some hours, for the forest undergrowth made clearing necessary, and we all worked strenuously with hatchets and *pangas*. Shorty felled several saplings with great rapidity and hacked his way vigorously into the bushes, pausing only to make a protest because it was Sunday. This was a day, he sometimes remembered, when labour was disapproved of by his church; but on this occasion he contented himself with working fully clad as a Sabbath touch. He was wearing a clean vest belonging to Michael, and the seat of his pants, which as usual was split apart from cheek to cheek, had been modestly drawn together with a safety-pin.

Before long the tents were erected in a leafy clearing, under enormous trees which spread hugely upwards like the roof of a cathedral. The sun could not penetrate here, and the place had an air of almost chilly solemnity. Everything, from the nearness of the river, was rank and green; where the trees ended a forest of reeds enclosed us, and from the trees themselves fans of orchids spread fingers among the moss of the high branches. It was like being in a cavern, with the sun blazing at the entrance and on the world outside, where life went on at a distance. There was no room in our dim interior for the kitchen camp, which was set up in the grass on the other side of the road, where it quickly became a centre of attraction. At no time of the day was it without visitors, usually women and girls who came with their waterpots and had a handful of eggs or a bunch of bananas to sell. The cook came into his own, being the only one of our three Africans who could understand something of the language, which was no longer Shona; he held court on a crate of bottles under the trees, bargaining for chickens.

He soon had several scrawny fowls in the dog-kennel and one or two others picking about in the road; Michael's biltong hung in strips from a tree. The camp had an established air, and felt like home. We wondered at first why we saw so few men, for nearly all the passers-by were women; but learned that this was a feature of native life in these parts, where the able-bodied males are rounded up for forced labour by the Portuguese. The husbands and sons of these women would be doing a three-year service, perhaps hundreds of miles away, on the roads or in the mines; the chiefs each year provided a quota of men as the price for continuing in tribal authority.

Next morning Michael was up with the lark, concentrating on his crocodile, which local information credited with taking a goat a fortnight, with having already survived two rifle wounds, and possessing great cunning. Michael was a little worried about the bullet holes, since these might have damaged the skin which he had already kindly offered me as a present; but he was full of optimism at breakfast, cleaning his rifle and studying his crocodile book, only too anxious that we should go off and amuse ourselves. This suited us well enough, for we were longing to return to Nyabánga, to form some idea of how best to explore the hill. We set off in the Land Rover, taking Peter's detour at the broken bridge and negotiating the gully at a shallower point without much difficulty. This new route took us through a group of native huts which struck us both by their poverty and by their lack of squalor. It was the home of a single family, a smallholding; everyone was gone for the day except an old man of extreme age who lay like a dried-up corpse at the door of his hut. He moved nothing but his eyes as we went through, and at the last moment returned our greeting with a fin-like movement of the hand. The hut beside which he lay, a frame of reeds and branches thatched with grass, was evidently the living-room of the family; we could see inside, and it was empty. The cooking hut, a roof supported on poles, had a fire in it, the smoke creeping slowly through the thatch. Here were a few cooking-pots of clay and a surrealist shape or two, scooped out from pumpkins into capacious ladles. Another hut was for storing water, and contained enormous clay jars and the carrying-pots which had not been taken to the river. A fourth hut, square in shape, was filled to the door with mealie cobs, and a fifth, not yet opened and smelling like the pit, was full of goats; we could see their beards and yellow eyes through the wattle. The striking thing about this place, which was as poor in possessions as any place could be, was the absence of all the dirt and litter that one

E

associates with 'civilized' poverty. Where nothing is bought and
life is supported wholly on what lives and grows, there is no
refuse; no empty tins, no dirty paper, no rubbish. The maize of
the mealies is eaten, the cobs are fuel. Where there is little,
everything is consumed. The only things we saw which presumably had not been made in the kraal were the scraps of cloth
round the old man's loins and the earth-coloured fragment of
blanket on which he lay. The huts themselves, being made of
branches and grass, were part of the hill, and their bareness gave
the place a formidable dignity.

The cattle-dip when we arrived was deserted, but there was a
battered lorry standing near the sheds, which we examined
warily from a distance. It had a Portuguese licence-plate, but
there was nothing to indicate whom it belonged to, nor why it
had come. We decided to climb the shallow stony hill which
ran down to the dip, to examine Nyabánga through field-glasses
and for a time at least to keep an eye on the lorry. Russell's
warning about Native Commissioners and their spies was never
far from our minds; we had not seen another vehicle since we left
Chikore, and were unwilling to approach Nyabánga with this
unexpected phenomenon unexplained. We left the Land Rover
at the bottom and went slowly up the eroded surface of the slope
which had been deeply corrugated by running water and pitted
by the hooves of innumerable cattle. On the crown of the slope
was a spinney of thin trees, and into this we withdrew for the
sake of a little shade and in order to use the field-glasses un-
observed. Though there was no one to be seen, not even a
child or a woman at the muddy stream, we had grown accustomed to the assumption that we were probably watched, and
acted on it; we should see some stealthy movement sooner or
later.

We sat for a long time in our screen of trees and studied what
our eyes could tell us of Nyabánga. On a ridge between the dip
and the rise of the hill the field-glasses showed the thatch of a
fair-sized kraal. This was either a small village or a homestead

bigger than any we had yet seen. No other habitation was distinguishable; so far as we could see the hill was neither cultivated nor inhabited; no mealie-patch, no roof, no path was visible. There was not a breath of wind, and the grass and trees, so deceptively looking like parched savannah through which one could walk at ease, gave off a still and burnished shine, and the edges of the hill quivered like sun-struck metal. It should not be difficult, we thought, to quarter the hills by degrees, looking for anything that might be a burial mound; but since much time must always be consumed in getting from the camp to the cattle-dip and negotiating the abominable rocks, it would be necessary to find a way of approaching much more closely in the Land Rover. If we could take the vehicle part-way up the hill the middle of the short day could be profitably spent, less valuable time wasted in coming and going. The physical difficulties of the climb seemed slight in comparison with the problem of explaining our strange preoccupation with the hill to Michael.

We lit a fire of twigs and made coffee, anxiously discussing the question of sharing our secret. Jack and Peter were less troubled perhaps than I was by the personal discomfort of keeping him in the dark, but they gloomily admitted all the practical difficulties. He could not be left indefinitely to hunt his crocodile while we disappeared daily to haunt this unprofitable place. His month's leave was nearly up, and if he were not to return to Salisbury without us we had got to work fast. Problem though he was, without him we should be barely able to communicate with our own Africans, and the thought of the Portuguese at Spungabera would be doubly uncomfortable. Besides, if we found what we were looking for on Nyabánga we should need all the help we could get; we should also need Shadow, who was the only efficient means we knew of keeping Africans at a distance. If we had to get out of this territory in a hurry we should do it better for not being a man short. In sum, and in spite of the hazards of his incalculable reaction, the story had got to be told. We needed Michael.

Drowsed by the heat and the complications of argument we one by one dropped out of the conversation, and putting a stone or a knapsack under our heads fell uncomfortably asleep. When we awoke the sun had travelled and a solitary man was standing beside the Land Rover. He was an African, but being neatly dressed in shorts and shirt with boots on he did not look like one of the local people. We gathered our things together and came slowly downhill, while he walked deliberately round the vehicle and appeared to be examining its licence-plates. We greeted him with upraised hand and voices that sounded more friendly than we felt, but he gave us no returning smile and said at once in English, 'Why you come?'

This did not sound like a purely social question, but Peter had the presence of mind to take it as such, and replied with affability that we were on holiday. The man frowned at this, and we could not tell whether he disliked or had merely misunderstood our answer. We stared at him in silence, and then Peter, beginning to suspect that his English was already exhausted, embarked on a further friendly conversation, waving his arms at random at the country, praising the beauty of the cattle-dip and showing him his camera. It was soon apparent that he understood little or nothing of what was said, and was less interested in us than in the Land Rover. We showed it gravely, opening the bonnet and inviting him to inspect the oily interior. He did not seem like an official, however humble, and we began to breathe again when he beckoned us across to look at his own lorry. It was battered, dirty and empty, and from the few words of English that he uttered we gathered that he was on his way to Chipinga. We could not learn where he came from; he may have been looking for company on the journey, and his air of frowning suspicion was perhaps no more than the reflection of his struggle with a foreign language. We pronounced the name 'Spungabera' in a questioning tone, but he shook his head; and after some more frowning and staring asked us with pointed gestures to give him some petrol.

Fortunately we had only a gallon in a spare tin, since he looked as though he were hoping for a large quantity, and this we obligingly poured into a crumpled container which he produced from the lorry. He offered us nothing in return and made no sign of continuing his journey. We left him at length, standing still and silent as we had first seen him, gazing moodily after us with a doubtful expression.

We went back to the camp with a troubled mind, anxious to ask Michael if he had seen this man, but as soon as we arrived at the river all thoughts of him were banished by a new difficulty. The crocodile had been given up as a bad job and Michael, presumably bored, had backed the lorry down the slope into the middle of the river. His intention had apparently been to give it a wash, but the current was stronger than he had imagined and the water deeper, and it was now wedged between slippery rocks, roaring its engine distressfully. He was not unduly worried, but was sitting in the cab as though on the bridge of a ship, shouting instructions to Shorty and John who were up to their thighs in water. He was unfeignedly pleased to see us, for he was sure that we could drag him out with chains. He had kept the engine running, since it had been incapable for a long time of starting without a tow, and he sent the *munts* scurrying to the Land Rover to attach him. Peter's face fell. He had long ago lost all confidence in the lorry, and was continually on the defensive against any schemes of Michael's which involved the Land Rover; he did not want, as he put it, its guts pulled out in a futile attempt to retrieve Michael's folly.

There was no alternative, however. The Land Rover was backed down the slope, where it clung at what looked like an angle of forty-five degrees, and was harnessed to the lorry with a double length of chain. With Michael and Peter at the wheels both motors were revved up to a deafening pitch, the Land Rover shuddered and groaned and threw out clods of earth from its heels like a dog, and the rest of us waded into the water and pushed; but nothing happened. The lorry's nose was pointed downwards against a rock and the bank was too steep for the Land Rover to lift it. After much uproar and struggling the lorry was allowed to relapse to its stertorous breathing and Michael and Shorty, both wet through and with teeth chattering with cold, fought to dislodge the frustrating rock with a crowbar. The sun had now set and it was fairly dark; a bank of cloud, the first we had seen, lay across the moon; we worked by the Land Rover's searchlight. Out of the darkness on either side a group of silent figures had now assembled, women, boys and old men. They stood at the top of the bank and sent up a faint cheer when the rock was finally prised from its foundations, the water swirling after it with a roar, and the lorry settled gratefully into the cavity. The extra strain imposed by this subsidence was too much for the chain, which at the next attempt broke in several places. The Land Rover rushed crossly up the bank dangling its fragments, and the lorry jerked its hindquarters sideways into a deeper and more comfortable position, where its lights continued to glow in and out to the rhythm of its heavy breathing. We had no ropes and no winch, and no amount of argument produced any better suggestion than that we should try to collect some extra men in the morning. The lorry's engine, at Michael's suggestion, was left running, for if it could not be started again a dead-weight of four tons would be hopeless; but to this the suffering mechanism was unequal; it had been running for hours and no one had looked at the tank. As we crawled wearily up the bank for the last time it coughed apologetically and was silent.

Messages were sent out next morning for extra men, and a couple of ragged ancients who had settled down with their staves at the side of the road, determined to miss nothing, assured us they would come; but after several hours of waiting no one appeared, and while Peter was off in the bush on some private occasion Michael removed the Land Rover's battery and transferred it to the lorry. It did not succeed in starting the lorry's motor, and when Peter furiously returned it to its proper place the Land Rover would not start either. It was pushed up the hill by hand until it recovered, then harnessed for a further attempt with pieces of rope and chain, but to no purpose; the tremors induced in the lorry shifted it with malicious skill into a worse position, so that it looked even more surely doomed than the night before, and as though it must stay in the river until it disintegrated.

We began to take a sombre view of our quandary, for if the lorry could not be moved, neither could the stores and camp equipment, and all seven of us would depend on the Land Rover. It would mean in effect the end of the expedition. Even Michael at last began to show signs of worry, for he was due to report in barracks in a few days' time, and did not like the idea of leaving us in Mozambique in this predicament. He would take the Land Rover, he said, and go back as far as Chipinga, where he could telephone his father and ask for an extension of leave; he would also take the lorry's battery and starter-motor, and if the battery would not hold a charge, borrow or hire another, or in the last resort buy one. The thought of being left without any means of moving was not pleasant, but we could think of no alternative. Michael took Shorty and Shadow with him for company, and being busy calculating our probable losses we saw him off without enthusiasm.

The next few days were spent in attempts to assuage a mounting feeling of frustration. Our time was slipping away; we were only seven miles from Nyabánga, and yet, without transport of any kind, we might as well have been fifty miles distant. To add fourteen miles a day on foot, in that heat, to the difficulties of exploring the hill itself, would have fatally consumed the daylight hours. The shortness of the day, which was never more nor less than twelve hours, was a nuisance to which we never grew accustomed. If we had been camped on the very skirts of Nyabánga the day would have been none too long for the climb and descent, with some interval between for searching and rest; with fourteen miles of rough bush trail besides, the thing was hopeless. We wildly considered, as the hours passed, whether we should try to carry our water and blankets and sleep on the hill, but the unknown hazards and the darkness were intimidating. We could see our whole plan collapsing because of this folly of the lorry, and ourselves perhaps stuck in this place indefinitely, or until the Portuguese came. One thing at least emerged with unpleasant sharpness; as soon as he returned, Michael must be let into the story.

As a parting kindness, and to keep us occupied, he had extracted a promise from one of the local ancients to show us the haunts of several near-by crocodiles; but needless to say this guide never appeared, and our only visitors were women with water-pots, incredulously amused at the sight of a white woman. We were not unduly sorry about the crocodile, being absorbed in our own problems; it seemed more important to survey the country as far as we were able, and to study Nyabánga from a distance. The best point for this was the crown of the nearest hill, which looked like a smaller version of Nyabánga, being covered with the same grass and stunted trees. It seemed easy, and there was no better way of passing the time than by climbing it several times by way of practice. We set off in the early afternoon of our first day of waiting, and had scarcely covered a quarter of a mile before we recognized an old and hateful illusion. The grass, which from a distance looked like sun-bleached meadow, was a dense forest of growth about eight feet high, springing up from a wicked confusion of earth and rock. One did not walk up the hill, one clung and scrambled, clutching at trees, stumbling in crevices, and all the time, because of the grass, maddeningly out of sight of one another. By the time we were two-thirds up the sun had set, and we had to tumble down again in a hurry. It was not an encouraging rehearsal for Nyabánga.

If it had not been for the frustration of being so idle, and our manifold anxieties, the place we were in would have afforded infinite pleasure. The river itself, as we followed its course through gorges of rock, through festoons of creeper and dream-like arcades of trees, was secretively beautiful; smooth volumes of yellow water poured and swirled between rocks on which butterflies rested, and monkeys fled shrieking before us in the high branches. The butterflies were large and flew with an air of languor at knee-level, settling on sequins of sunlight among the stones. The commonest were brown and spotted like guinea-fowl, and there were many of Chinese blue with stripes of black and yellow at the tips of the wings, and an even larger apparition of black velvet which sailed idly before us as we advanced, as though offering itself to the net. We saw few huts in our wanderings and fewer people; only at the drift, when we returned, would there be a handful of goats brought down to drink, driven by little boys with musical instruments.

The sounds these made were monotonous and sweet, and carried on the still air to a great distance. One was an empty gourd, into which the player blew a hollow note. Another was a child's approach to the idea of a fiddle, a bow of hardwood notched from end to end and strung with a ribbon of grass. One end of the bow was placed against the mouth, and while the player sang through his teeth he stridulated against the notches with a little stick which carried a gourd full of beans at one end, like a rattle. It was music which might have been made by a child playing in consort with a grasshopper. The most ambitious instrument we saw was carried by older boys and was clearly a prized possession. It was a little zither made from a square of wood, the inside hollowed out for a sounding-board and the keys made of iron nails, curved and flattened. When a curved point was depressed by a finger, it sprang back into shape with a clear note, and since the nails were carefully graded in length it was possible to play between five and a dozen notes of a faulty scale. The most satisfactory tones were the ones most used, and three- and five-note tunes were varied endlessly. We heard one other instrument besides these, on a day when we waded across the river and went for a long day's walk into the hills, but there was nobody near it and we had to play it ourselves. We found it in a clearing beside the ashes of a fire, and since the ground was sprinkled with goat-droppings we guessed that this was a place the herd-boys used. The instrument was a little hollow scooped out of the earth, carefully lined with trusses of dried grass. On either side a wooden trestle was fixed, about three inches high, and across these several pieces of hard red wood, carefully smoothed and graded in length, had been pegged in place. The sticks for playing this xylophone or drum were lying across it, as though left for the next session, and we amused ourselves for a while in the shade by playing variations on its light, dry, curiously resonant notes.

As the sky piled up with incandescent cloud the haze on the distant hilltops vanished and their outlines took on the hardness of blue crystal. The children's music by the river, coming and going in the evening with their goats, was like the clicking of insects and the cries of birds, with the bell-like note of the zither, its surest one, repeated endlessly like the sound one hears in a cave of dropping water. An unseen bird high in our cathedral roof punctuated the theme with his own persistent statement, a loud dry click like striking a key on a typewriter, followed at once by a long and liquid note. The whole chorus was complex and clear, heard through a limpid atmosphere which already carried the promise of coming rain.

The rain began at dawn the following day, splashing in sudden heavy drops on my face and spreading a noisy patter through the trees. I was wet through before I could get my blankets into the tent, and before it was light the hard earth of the camp had turned to mud. There was no wind; the rain fell in rods from a dark sky, unvarying in sound and volume for eight hours. Our fire hissed and steamed and was finally quenched; the road turned to slime and the slope leading down to the river became a slide. Our poor Africans crouched in misery under the lorry's canvas, spread over themselves and the stores, and we lay on our beds despondently through the day, rousing ourselves at intervals to eat depressing meals out of wet tins. The river began to rise, and by evening, when the rain stopped, was well above the lorry's axles, flowing fast under the body of the truck. The moon came out among ragged clouds and I shivered in a wet bed by a dead fire, the trees dripping despondently on my pillow.

The next day was dark and threatening, with mist and cloud spread thickly over the valley. There was no wind and little movement; only the river was lively, pouring round and under the wrecked lorry; from time to time a cloud on the hill unfolded a long and weeping streamer of rain. We were too restless and anxious to wait any longer where we were, watching the lorry drown, and set off to walk to the cattle-dip to meet Michael. The air was still and heavy and full of moisture, laden with new and aromatic smells. Everything had come to life in the wake of the storm; great ants were abroad on the road in glistening armies, deploying their columns in complicated manœuvres; the rustle of their feet on the leaves was faintly audible. Butterflies clustered like flowers on a fragment of carrion, and thick black seven-inch millipedes travelled recklessly before us on the path, transforming themselves into ammonites at a touch. The muddy chine where the lorry had had so much trouble was carved into new rivulets by the rain; we covered its slopes with branches, fearing for the Land Rover. It had been one of Michael's intentions to call on Hla-Hla, in the hope that he could send a tractor to haul out the lorry, but we listened for the sound of a diesel engine in vain. Only at one point, when we stopped to dig the clay off our boots with a stick, we heard women's voices at a distance, high and clear in the thicket like the voices of birds. We were sitting on a fallen tree and they were unaware of us, coming down the wooded hillside chattering and laughing; as they drew near we saw that they were carrying pieces of freshly cut timber on their heads. They saw us in the same instant and were suddenly silent, standing frozen like deer behind a screen of trees, and neither spoke nor stirred until we moved on. Then the bird-like chatter broke out again, softly and cautiously, but so long as we were in sight they did not appear.

We spent several fruitless hours at the cattle-dip, not daring to go farther for fear of missing Michael, gazing despondently at Nyabánga, now shrouded and remote in heavy cloud. We had been nearly a week in this place, and the hill itself seemed farther off than ever. If only the clouds would break and the sun come out; if only the ground would dry and Michael return; if only the lorry were out of the river and all of us escaped from the *cul-de-sac* in which it had trapped us . . .

But at this point the rain began again, spreading a network of rivulets over the road and making the going so slippery that it took several miserable hours to return, helping ourselves with sticks and grotesquely slithering about in clay and débris.

8

The Magic and the Hill

By the time it was fully dark an arena of clear sky had opened above us and the moon was rising majestically bright. It was once more nearing the full; everything was clear and strange under that marvellous radiance, reminding us of something nearly incredible—that we had already been a whole month in the bush. As we approached the camp we heard the jerky roar of the Land Rover crossing the rocks, and presently Michael overtook us. He was in good spirits; his father had obtained him a week's extension of leave, the lorry's starter-motor had been doctored in Chipinga and the battery recharged, and he had hired a medieval-looking contraption which he said was a winch and which looked as though it had come out of a torture-chamber. This heavy ratcheted machine was equipped with an old steel hawser and lengths of chain; only the rack was missing.

He was confident that it would pull the lorry out of the river in the morning.

This was the occasion, as we dried our sodden clothes at the hissing fire, when we should have made a clean breast of everything to Michael, but a gloomy apprehension was still on us, and we said nothing. We did not share his trust in the ugly winch, and had a pessimistic feeling that if this also failed, and the only remaining hope was Hla-Hla's tractor, we might well be there for another week on the river. It would be time enough to tell him when the future seemed less hopeless than it did now; time was running out for all of us, and we secretly blamed him for the wreck of the expedition. It was even a final exasperation that he had not thought it necessary to call on Hla-Hla, so great was his new-found confidence in the winch. The rain, he said, had been a fluke; such a thing had never been heard of at this season. An hour or two of sun and the ground would be dry; he would winch the lorry out for us in the morning.

I was wakened again before dawn by sudden rain, but it was less resolute than before and there were watery gleams of sun an hour later. The winch was lashed with rope to a stout tree and Michael and the *munts* slithered up and down the disintegrating slope, replacing the starter-motor and battery in the lorry. The engine, to no one's surprise but Michael's, refused to start. The winch was manned, but its hawser proved too short to reach the lorry and there was no other tree in a practicable position. The pieces of chain which had come with the winch were contemptible, and had to be lashed together with pieces of rope. As soon as the lorry was harnessed the ropes broke, and we spent some hours in scouring about for native bullock-chains, used for dragging heavy sledges and timber. These when found were ingeniously hooked together and miraculously held, but as soon as the winch was started it broke in two, revealing an old encrusted break which in some remote age had been incompetently welded. That was the end of the winch and of our hopes for the lorry; we sat on the edge of the road with our heads in our hands. This is a good position for constructive thought, and after a time two rather doubtful ideas presented themselves. Michael would send a message to the Portuguese chief, asking for help, and we three would go back in the Land Rover to Hla-Hla. If Hla-Hla would send us his tractor, and the tractor could reach us, we had a chance; but we also had a private and ulterior motive. If we could find Zamchiya as well, and he would allow us to camp in his kraal at the cattle-dip, we might, even without the lorry, be within reasonable striking distance of Nyabánga and could pass the time of waiting in reconnaissance. We did not mention this to Michael, since our obsession with the hill would need explaining, and we had a sufficient motive in the tractor. Michael wrote a lordly request for fifty men, carefully printed in Shona in thick pencil, and before we left we had the exquisite pleasure of seeing the note carried off in a cleft stick. This was something we had never expected to see outside, perhaps, the pages of Evelyn Waugh; but there it was, being done as a matter of course, and the youth who had been found to carry it forded the river and ran off with it held at arm's length, like a banner.

When we had made the usual painful course to the cattle-dip we found that it was dipping day, and the place was crowded with cattle as though it were a fair. Herds were converging on the dip from every direction, driven by boys armed with bamboo poles. We watched them for a while, surprised at the docile behaviour of the long-horned beasts, which were driven one by one into a narrow passage and plunged over head and eyes in the stinking trough. There was much shouting, but none of that orgiastic beating of animals which is the horror of cattle fairs in European countries; a light whack with the bamboo was all that was needed, and only the calves panicked and thrashed about, and had to be guided out of the bath with poles.

So far as we could remember this was one of the days when Zamchiya was due at the cattle-dip, to hold his weekly session of Chief Law, and it seemed sensible that I should wait for him here while Jack and Peter went on to look for Hla-Hla. Left alone at the dip I made my way to the kraal we had seen from the hill; it was the only one we knew of, and we supposed it to be Zamchiya's, but only women and children were there and most of them fled at the sight of me. I tried Zamchiya's name on those that remained, but either it meant nothing to them or they were startled into speechlessness by my appearance, for however I tried the question they remained equally silent and amazed. There was nothing for it but to wait for the others to return, and I wandered off to a bare mound where I had a view of the cattle-dip, and sat under the tree growing out of the crown of it, idly whittling a gourd I had picked up by the river. Here I was some-what beset by little boys, who played an elaborate hide-and-seek round the foot of the ant-hill, fleeing in terror whenever I looked or spoke, and then peeping out of the bushes, all eyes and smiles. Presently a man came down from the kraal and approached me. He looked handsome and prosperous, and had a pink knitted woollen cap on the back of his head. This he courteously re-moved when we were within speaking distance, and asked me some question, to which I could only reply by shrugging and smiling. He had no fewer than five gold rings on his fingers, and one of the rings was crudely set with a diamond. We could not understand one another, and after more smiling and gesturing we nodded a friendly farewell and he went away. He was followed after an interval by a woman who seemed not at all afraid of me, but even extravagantly delighted with the encounter. She set down her water-pot, the better to talk and laugh and wave her arms, and I responded as best I could, laying down my knife and pumpkin for the purpose. It was puzzling that neither of them seemed to respond to the name of Zamchiya.

When Jack and Peter returned it was with the good news that Hla-Hla's tractor was already on the way. It was a powerful Ferguson and had good chains; if it could manage the gullies on the trail the situation was promising. They had also seen

Zamchiya, who had made them a further handsome present of
naartjes, but he had seemed preoccupied that morning, and they
had had a strong feeling that it would have been unpropitious
to ask about sleeping in his huts. If the tractor failed, there was
still this last resort; there was something about Zamchiya's gaze
which had made them uncomfortable.

As we stood talking the tractor appeared, manned by a
spirited driver in a raffia hat, and went boldly on ahead of us
down the trail. Jack had been looking at Nyabánga through the
field-glasses, and now said that he would like to give the rest of
the day to exploring it on foot, having long had the feeling that
we should get very little nearer to it with the Land Rover. If he
could find a negotiable path to the summit much time would be
saved, and such knowledge as he could gain would be useful
later. He accordingly went off by himself, crossing the muddy
stream in the direction of the hill, and Peter and I drove hopefully
after the tractor.

We found it where we might have known we should, at the
bottom of the chine. Its enormous wheels, armoured with great
corrugated tyres, were churning up the sides of the gully like
butter, making sidelong rushes at the face and sliding down
again. The driver was full of resource and enthusiasm and was
enjoying himself; he did not pause in his plunging backwards and
forwards until the whole of the farther slope had been reduced to
a welter of furrows streaming with water. He then got out of the
saddle, laughing heartily, and beckoned to four old men who had
appeared like spirits with *pangas* out of the wood. Between
them they hacked down a quantity of brushwood and packed it
thickly into the slimy grooves, making a temporary surface of
which Peter took advantage in the Land Rover, tearing sideways up the side of the chine like a crab; but it did nothing to
help the tractor. This was clearly another case for chains, and
we left the five Africans laughing and chattering over the
plight of the tractor while we went on in the direction of
the camp to see what we could find. Hla-Hla's machine had

fallen into the trap like an elephant into a pit, but at least its engine was running and it was not up to the floorboards in the river.

When we reached the camp we stopped abruptly in amazement: the place was crowded with people. Michael was standing in a thick knot of men whom we had not seen before, and there was another group on the far side of the river. The Portuguese chief had come, having heard what happened a full day before Michael had sent his message; he had decided to investigate, and had in fact encountered our messenger when he was only a few miles from the Umzilizwe. Michael drew us aside at once and warned us in an undertone that the proceedings were likely to be long-drawn and formal. The Chief was an important one, and protocol would have to be observed. It was particularly desirable, he said anxiously, that I should keep in the background, for the Chief would not care to be spoken to by a woman.

Peter and I withdrew discreetly under a tree, where we could watch the proceedings, and word was passed to the Chief on the other side of the river that Michael was now ready to receive him. A small old man now detached himself from the group and was ceremoniously lifted on to the back of one of his companions and carried in this position over the river, the rest of the company wading respectfully behind him. He stopped when he was a dozen yards from Michael and made a signal that he was ready to sit. Two of our battered camp chairs were now brought for the principals, and he and Michael sat facing one another at what seemed to us an inconvenient distance, but it appeared that this was simply a matter of formality, since it would not be proper for them to converse directly. The Chief spoke into the ear of his eldest son, who bent solicitously to receive instructions and passed them on in turn to a lesser dignitary, who then transferred the message to our cook, who translated it into Shona to John and Shorty. They then, being fully conversant with the system of chain-communication suitable to a chief's dignity, passed on the message to Michael sitting in his chair, whose reply was conveyed back in the same manner. A conversation conducted in this fashion is a slow business, but such grave satisfaction was expressed on the faces of the crowd that one could not have wished to see it done more quickly. The gist of the exchange, as we afterwards learned from Michael, was that the Chief was willing to help us out of our difficulty, provided that it was our intention to proceed afterwards to Spungabera and report our presence and our business to the Portuguese. He himself, he said, would be obliged to report the matter to the Native Commissioner, and without this understanding nothing could be done, since he was answerable to the Portuguese and they were well known to be interested in strangers. This was a facer for Michael, but fortunately he was not troubled by scruples, least of all where the Portuguese were concerned, and replied gravely that we were indeed on our way to Spungabera, where we looked forward to paying the Native Commissioner a visit. In that case, said the Chief, would it not be well to take the lorry out on the farther side, and carry the other vehicle over as well, and our stores, so that we could proceed on our journey? By a happy chance Michael did not agree to this, for though he knew nothing of our real plans, at least he knew that having crossed the border already without permission, nothing would be farther from our thoughts than Spungabera. So he said no, for the present we wished to stay on this side of the river, as he had Europeans from England in his party, who had arranged to have private talks with Chief Zamchiya. This appeared to give satisfaction: the Chief conferred with his elders, and word was passed that they would need two shillings. Four sixpences were found in Peter's pocket and the money changed hands; it was not, we learned from our interpreters, to be regarded as a fee, but for the purchase of a sacrificial chicken. There was some delay before the chicken was forthcoming; Michael and the Chief sat patiently in their chairs while the crowd conversed in whispers. At last a child arrived carrying a fowl by the legs, and the

Chief announced that he and his elders would now re-cross the river. Before mounting his bearer, however, he passed a courteous message to Michael, inviting him to accompany them. He had taken a fancy to Michael, he said, and was willing that he should witness the necessary ceremonies from a distance.

Michael accepted after a momentary hesitation, caused by his fear of losing face if he waded through the river on his own legs; but it was no good thinking that Shorty could make a dignified job of carrying him, so he compromised by not removing his boots. The Chief was carried over dry-shod, preceded by his elders, with Michael floundering powerfully in his wake, and the rest of us gathered on the muddy bank above the lorry to watch developments.

Arrived on the other side the elders withdrew with the chicken under a tree, and the Chief motioned to Michael to stand with him in a privileged group at a little distance. It was not possible, he said, still conveying his meaning through a chain of intermediaries, for a European to watch their magic too closely. The purpose of the ceremony was to draw power from the spirits of their ancestors who had been devoured by the crocodile in this very river; it was to the malign influence of the crocodile that we could attribute even this disaster to our lorry. The elders by this time were crouching under their tree; there was a brief squawk and no more was heard of the chicken. There was muttering and a weird singing that sounded like mooing, and then the whole party slowly recrossed the river.

The Chief had brought thirty-four men with him, and these were now divided into two groups. Twenty went into the water on either side of the lorry, and fourteen ranged themselves on top of the bank. The twenty put their hands to the lorry and waited, and at a signal from the Chief the others began to sing. The song, as Michael translated it, began with a rousing imperative – 'Let us show how strong our warriors are!' and went on into swinging verses something like this:

'Ho, ho, men!
Come on, men!
We are not women,
Heave . . .'

Each time on the '*Heave!*' the twenty shouldered the lorry, and
each time their combined strength urged it perceptibly forward
over the rocks. With each verse the singing grew wilder and
louder, and Shadow slunk in terror into the bush. When they
came to the final submerged rock, which was immovable, the
singers leaped in the air with huge cries, and first the front of
the lorry and then the tail were lifted clean over it. It came out on
the bank, dripping with weed and water like a river monster,
and was sung and heaved right up the slippery slope. The
crowd burst out into wild cheering and excitement and the lorry
was patted and stroked by scores of hands, as though it too had a
share in the achievement.

Michael made elaborate thanks through the proper channels
and then asked what present he might make in return for this
kindness. For each of his men, the Chief replied, a shilling would
be handsome compensation; for himself five rounds of buckshot
would be acceptable. He was too grand to receive these things
into his own hand, and made a stately return across the river
while we were frantically going through our pockets for silver.
As a parting civility he invited Michael to bring 'his people' to a
party which he would give for us, with beer and singing, when
we reached his kraal on our way to Spungabera.

The rest of the day was given over to modest festivities, for
so stirring an occasion could not be relinquished lightly, and
most of the Chief's people remained to celebrate. Tinned fruit
and tinned beer (a poor offering, but they were accepted as rare
delicacies) were doled out in small quantities, and when these
were finished the heroes willingly posed for a group photograph.
The power they had received from their ancestors was still
working in them, urging them to further feats, and a dozen of

them went off to the broken bridge and set about repairing it. The speed with which they accomplished this, cutting down trees and branches with hatchets and *pangas*, seemed to us no less magical than the rescue of the lorry; they were exalted in spirit and seemed capable of anything. We even thought of taking them back to the chine to lift out the tractor, but when Jack arrived at the camp, dusty and footsore, he announced that the thing had somehow got out on its own side; he had met it ploughing home in the direction of Hla-Hla.

Jack had his own news to give us, for he had actually been to the top of Nyabánga. It had been difficult, he said, but the thing could be done, though he doubted whether any of it would be possible for the Land Rover. He had followed false trails and been lost in some thorny thickets, but thought he might remember the route which had been at last successful. The hill was bigger than we had thought and the bush very dense; after some mealie-patches on the lower slopes there had been no sign of habitation. His climb was passed off as an 'interesting walk', since Michael was with us, sipping an unaccustomed whisky in honour of the day's triumph, stretching out his great legs before the fire and basking in the return of mutual benevolence.

It had indeed been a wonderful day; the spell of ill-luck had been broken by one more potent, the lorry was safe, the bridge had been rebuilt, and there was nothing (except perhaps the condition of the chine) to prevent our moving camp the next morning. Never can the sacrifice of a fowl have been more profitable. And as if to set a seal on the day and mark it as one of plenitude, a girl arrived in the camp as we sat round the fire, bearing on her head a great pot of wild honey. She had brought it to sell, asking only a few shillings for the contents of the jar, which must have contained not less than sixteen pounds. She was an elegant creature of about seventeen, with ankles encased in bracelets of metal wire extending like greaves almost to the bend of the knee; her neck was garlanded with strings of beads and she wore a police whistle on a string. (She explained, when asked, that she was accustomed to play this instrument at dances.) She set down the pot at our feet and took off the covering of dried banana-leaf which had been tied in place with strands of twisted bark. It was full to the brim with honey, a gleaming mass floating with broken comb, and gave off a heavy smell of powerful sweetness. We tasted it at once with a spoon, lifting the dripping fragments to our mouths and crushing the fragile complex with our teeth. Whenever the spoon broke the comby surface the dark honey welled up like flowing topaz, bringing the dark bodies of drowned bees. It was stronger than any honey I had ever tasted, its sweetness streaked with a lingering memory of wood-smoke, as though it had been taken that very day from the hive. We had seen native beehives here and there, beautifully constructed cylinders of curved bark, fastened together with wooden pegs, lodged high above the ground in a likely tree. I am not clear why the appearance and taste of this honey was so moving, but it seemed to contain a strong and mysterious element, as though it were part of the substance of life itself, and we ate it in silence, passing the spoon gravely from hand to hand. It was a strange thing to burden ourselves with at this stage, enormously heavy and the pot round-bottomed so that it could not stand upright, but it had come like a final grace on a day of blessing, and we gratefully put the silver in the girl's hand.

The last undertaking of the day was to tell Michael everything that we had so far concealed, and to this my guilty nerves proved unequal. I dreaded his reaction, could not tell for a moment how he would take it, and feared that this, and not the accident to the lorry, would be the ultimate undoing of the expedition. I was incapable of sitting quietly by the fire, watching Michael's face while the story was unfolded, and retired cravenly into our tent with a book and a candle, leaving the men to themselves and trying not to listen to the murmur of voices.

They talked for a long time: I could distinguish Jack's steady tones, with brief pauses when Michael asked a question, but I could not interpret the drift of the conversation. There was no way of bearing the suspense but to be out of earshot, and I soon blew out the candle, lifted the flap of the tent, and wandered down to the edge of the moonlit river. I have no skill in judging character on short acquaintance, and though Michael's company delighted me and he seemed on the surface to be as transparent as the day, I guessed that there might be hidden reefs of obstinacy. His nature seemed to be one of innocence and good humour, with that reckless carelessness which comes from physical splendour and lack of thought. He was gentle in manner and full of intolerant opinions; there was much in him to which I was a stranger. His Rhodesian upbringing had filled him with simple bigotry, with a lordly belief in the white man and a contempt for the black which was total and instinctive; he had evidently responded with zest to police training. What we were proposing to do might affront or alarm him; he might be the wrong sort of person for such a venture, too disciplined, too puritanical, or both. Nevertheless some communion of sympathy told me that under the correct exterior lurked the instincts of a poacher.

When I came slowly back from the river it was all over. The three were at ease with their boots stretched to the fire and Michael made only a dream-like movement to make room for me, so deep was he in the discussion of the cunning strategy to follow when we had found the diamonds. He had responded wholly, as we all had in the beginning, to the glittering vision of Umzila's treasure, and felt none of the misgivings that had worried us later. Africa was full of such hoards, he said; a few of them came to light from time to time, and people had had their throats cut who were caught looking for them. If any of the chiefs in this part knew of the treasure we would certainly be watched, and if our Africans got any inkling of it they would be off into the bush in a flash; there was no act so dangerous as to violate a grave. He had some ominous stories to tell us of past prospectors, whose limbs had been hung like biltong from the branches, and was scarcely more reassuring when he recounted some anecdotes of the Portuguese police, with whose methods he was familiar; but none of these considerations seemed to daunt him; he was as much our man as if he had been a brother.

He knew something of African burial customs, and was able to confirm all we had learned from Russell and the missionaries. The undistinguished dead were simply put into the ground and their graves forgotten; only a chief's resting-place would be marked by a mound and possibly a tree, and would be tended for perhaps a generation. After that the site itself would be forgotten by all but a few old men who would keep the secret, and the place would be avoided and feared as the abode of spirits. Nothing in our story struck Michael as being in the least unlikely; what worried him (as indeed it worried us to the point of not wishing to think about it) was what we should do with the treasure if we found it. He now saw the disaster of the lorry in its true light; nothing could have served better to publicise our presence in the area; it would be known for miles around that we were there, and the news might already have reached Spungabera. If we were to make our search before the Portuguese arrived, as he was sure they eventually would, we had got to work fast, and our first necessity was to camp as near as possible to Nyabánga. We could not camp at the cattle-dip, it was too public, but we thought that by following the river a little farther along we might find a place with cleaner water, which for a few nights at least would serve our purpose. From there we could explore the hill, and if we found a likely spot would dig as fast and as secretly as we could. After that, whether we found anything or not we would have to get out, and quickly; it would be madness to linger on the hill once the news leaked out that we were digging. If we found nothing, a rapid getaway would be essential, for apart from the African reaction the Portuguese would not take kindly to our unlawful entry, and we did not wish to be escorted to Spungabera by the police. If, on the other hand, we were successful, the situation would be a thousand times more dangerous; there would not be a moment to be lost, and we would have to have a plan to cover our retreat.

We had given this a good deal of nervous thought, and it was a great relief to be able to discuss it with Michael, since he after all knew the country as we did not, and besides was a policeman. The plan took shape round the fire that night as though we were planning the action of a crime novel. We would concentrate solely on the diamonds, which could easily be distributed among our pockets, and would make the best speed we could out of Mozambique and straight through, driving night and day, to Salisbury. Here we would take the first available plane, either together or separately, ostensibly flying to London. Jack in fact would fly straight through, but either Peter or I, or both, would stop over in Rome, carrying the diamonds on us and getting the earliest flight we could for Antwerp. Friends with respectable contacts with the diamond market had told us, when discreetly questioned months before, that Antwerp and not Amsterdam was the centre. It would not be difficult to find brokers who were more interested in uncut stones than in their place of origin, and it would be perfectly proper to leave a sealed box in a safe deposit. Once that was done, we could make our way back to London at our leisure, and months afterwards, if need be, if there had been no repercussions from the Portuguese or from Rhodesia, we could go back quietly to Antwerp and dispose of the stones discreetly through the regular channels.

It seemed very strange to be making such bizarre plans, sitting round a glowing fire in the leafy dark, and when panic occasionally ran through my nerves like a shudder I took comfort in the thought that it was probable, after all, that we should find nothing. Yet the possibility of success was also a real one, and in the trembling firelight we felt very close to it. It was a marvellous night, still and rather cold, and the dazzling effulgence of the moon, which had reached the full, pierced our cathedral roof with a thousand sequins. The smoke from our fire rose up in a soft column, filtering slowly through the leafy canopy to emerge with a ghostly radiance of its own. Michael and I lay awake for a long time by the fire, exchanging desultory and ever drowsier sentences, until I dreamed that we were digging in an earth tunnel, in a cold smell which I knew was the smell of bones.

Next morning early, anxious to lose no time, we left the packing up of the camp to the boys and set out in the Land Rover with food and water. It was our plan to make a preliminary survey of the hill, so as not to lose a day in moving camp, and to shift to our new quarters the following morning. We crossed the stream at the cattle-dip, passed the kraal which I had already visited and bumped over the rutted trail until it came to an end at a trampled and muddy watering-place. From here the grass and trees were too thick for the Land Rover and we set out on foot, searching for the thread-like trail which had eventually taken Jack to the summit of the hill; but whenever we found one (and there were many, criss-crossing through the high grass like the paths that a colony of ants might make in a hayfield) it meandered aimlessly hither and thither, ending after half a mile at a tattered mealie-patch or petering out at a hole or a straggle of pumpkins. Once in the grass we could not see the hill, though whenever the paths led on to higher ground we caught baffling glimpses of it, never the same and always changing its position. It was not, of course, the simple feature that it seemed, for no sooner had we climbed for an encouraging distance than the ground would fall away into a tangled valley, thick with thorns and reeds and knotted creepers through which we struggled painfully, using our knives, before we could begin to ascend the hill again. Jack was determined to find his yesterday's path, which was somewhere in this malicious maze and which he had marked by knotting tussocks of grass, but Michael soon grew impatient of the search and was sure we should do better by fixing our position with compasses and cutting our way remorselessly uphill. We split into two pairs on this suggestion, Jack and Peter continuing their search and Michael and I plunging straight into the grass thicket. Our progress through this jungle was inconceivably slow, for even Michael was submerged and we only occasionally caught a glimpse of the summit, so that when we eventually came out on the edge of an unexpected kraal the hill was nowhere to be seen and we found we had lost our bearings altogether. The group of huts appeared as usual to be deserted, and as we wandered through it we noticed a peculiar feature. This was a circle of ground like a small garden, outlined by stones and enclosed by handsome trees. The ground was smooth and even appeared to be swept, and a flowering bush had been planted in the centre. Three metal tool-heads had been stuck upright in the ground under this bush, and a yard away from it some straight and forked sticks had been planted in the earth, forming a rectangle. We stood mutely staring at these strange signs, and the same discouraging thought occurred to both of us. Was it possible that we had stumbled on what we were looking for, and that this tended place marked an important grave? We were soberly considering this possibility when a young girl came out of one of the huts, appearing unpleasantly startled at the sight of us. Michael spoke reassuringly in Shona and she came a little closer, pleating the folds of her beaded kilt in her fingers. She understood him well enough and replied timidly, pointing with a long black arm and giving us clear directions for the top of the hill, but when we asked her what the 'garden' was she looked frightened and said (which seemed unlikely) that she did not know. Michael pressed his question, saying that the garden was pretty, and eventually, after glancing in every direction but ours, she ran away into the hut and fetched an older woman who might have been her mother. The woman listened with downcast eyes to a repetition of the question, and replied in a musical sing-song voice that the garden marked the site of a big hut which had fallen down long ago. We asked who had lived in the hut but she did not remember, and as to the rectangle of sticks, they were apparently as much of a puzzle to her as they were to us. Somebody must have put them there, she said helpfully. Perhaps it was children.

This could have been the truth, but we were uneasy, for if it were not, we should make no headway against this bland concealment, and if it were indeed Umzila's grave, the thought of digging in a populated kraal was plainly ludicrous. We took careful note of the position of the place, exchanged courtesies, and went on in the direction of the hill.

The trail the girl had indicated was the right one; half an hour's further climbing brought us to the very spot that Jack had described, a clearing in the grass and trees that had been used for wood-cutting. There were several stacks of timber there, drying in the sun, and a small thatched shelter such as the herd-boys used, in the shade of which we found Jack and Peter asleep. They had succeeded at last in finding Jack's fugitive path and had reached the top an hour ago, but had been too hot and tired to explore farther.

From the open patch round the little shelter we could see across a panorama of hills, but on every other side the tangle of grass and trees enclosed us like a wall. When we had eaten and rested we began to skirmish about for a better view, and digested the difficult nature of the summit. It was more extensive than we had supposed, and the trees, which were a scrub growth extending leafy branches out of the eight-foot grass, were dense enough to prevent our seeing anything, and at the same time not big enough to be climbed. I made several attempts, being the lightest of the four, but all that happened was that I found myself enclosed in a cage of leaves, and the lens-hood was scraped off my camera and swallowed irretrievably by the grass. Again we divided, determined to make some attempt to quarter the hill, each one of us cutting a path in a different direction; but after an hour of this arm-breaking work Michael and I had found only more trees, more grass, more thorns, and had torn our skin and clothes fairly extensively. Peter and Jack came back with something better: they had made their way to the one big tree we had seen so many times on the crown of Nyabánga, and reported that it was of considerable size, of a kind they thought we had none of us seen before, and growing out of a mound of striking proportions.

This was exciting news, and Michael and I were eager to see it for ourselves, but as usual there was no time for further search. It was past three o'clock; in less than two hours the sun would set, and half an hour after that it would be dark. We had no wish to be benighted on the hill, and it was important besides to find a better way down. Peter and Jack had lost much time before they had hit the trail, and Michael and I had made many wasteful traverses. We agreed that it was vital to find a way for the Land Rover at least through the bush surrounding the hill, otherwise too much daylight and energy would always be spent in the toil of merely getting up and down, with no time left for searching, let alone digging. Jack had his own ideas of the best route to take, and so, as usual, had Michael. Once more we divided, so as to cover the great number of possibilities, each pair heading for where we supposed the watering-place to be, where we had left the Land Rover. As it turned out, Jack's sense of direction was the better of the two; he and Peter were back at the Land Rover in little more than an hour, while Michael and I got badly lost, spending two and a half hours following false trails and cutting our way through cane-brakes, and when we eventually reached level ground we were a couple of miles towards the wrong side of the hill, and had to do some more dejected walking.

Michael was still fresh though he looked disreputable, but I was worn out and my left foot had blistered, my hateful boots having once more done their work. Our clothes had been torn in several places and our arms and Michael's knees were crusted with blood. We had cut ourselves stout sticks on the way down, and with these and Michael's scrubby beard and my dirty knapsack we made a pair of very sordid figures. We trudged on doggedly, scarcely speaking now that we were sure of our direction, and were presently startled to see two strange Africans, also with sticks and also carrying bundles, coming along the trail as though to meet us. Michael raised his hand to pass them with the usual curt salute when to our surprise they caught our hands and warmly wrung them, laughing with pleasure and clapping our arms and shoulders in boisterous greeting. Poor Michael all but reeled with horror at the contact, snatching back the hand that never touched a black one, but (for my sake, I think) swallowing the proper reply to such impertinence. He stood still and listened scowling while the two men burst into a torrent of conversation. His replies were short and I could see that he was not pleased, but I had no idea of the extent of the insult he was suffering until our hands had once more been vigorously shaken and the travellers had gone their way.

'What was that all about, Michael? Who on earth are they?'

'Just a couple of — *munts*, on their way somewhere.'

'But why were they so pleased to see us? What did they say?'

'I'm afraid they took us for poor whites. They thought we were travelling on foot, as they were. They told us there were huts at the cattle-dip, where we could sleep.'

I was delighted with this glimpse of ourselves through other eyes, but Michael at first was anything but amused. He strode along, making me trot to keep up, murmuring, 'Poor whites!' amazedly under his breath. I could see that we presented a shabby appearance and anywhere else might well have been taken for tramps, but I had missed the finer points of the Africans' judgement. In the first place, Michael said, when he had calmed down sufficiently, it was unheard-of for Europeans to travel on foot. Only Africans did that, and those occasional lost characters whom everyone despised, who scratched a living here and there in Africa and were contemptuously known and tolerated as 'poor whites'. The fact that I was the one who was carrying a knap-sack, and had been limping behind Michael on the narrow trail, would have perfectly fitted in with this impression, for in the native world it is woman who carries the burdens. The rough staves we plodded with and Michael's beard had all been part of the picture, and consequently the friendly strangers had not been afraid of us. We both looked so travel-stained and I so footsore that in the kindness of their hearts they had been glad to tell us there were native huts ahead. When presently we met a string of women with water-pots and one of them respectfully offered Michael a drink, he began to feel better, but a certain disenchantment with his beard dated from this incident.

9
The Drums Begin

FOR our final camp we were determined to settle as near to Nyabánga as possible; provided we had water we did not care how little there was, nor how much the *munts* complained; now that Michael's authority was behind us there was not likely to be much trouble from that quarter. Both vehicles, creeping like snails, got over the bridge without accident, the heavy load of equipment going over by hand. Both were unloaded again at the chine as a precaution, and the Land Rover scrambled through on a bed of branches. The lorry gave us some anxious moments, for the furrows cut by the tractor were not yet dry and the wheels spun into the soft clay like butter; but after hacking branches until we were tired somebody had the brainwave of using the barbecue, and this long-suffering object, which had made our toast and added a smoky touch to so many meals, was put under the wheels of the lorry and brought it out of the chine with a roar of triumph.

We passed the cattle-dip and went on for perhaps a quarter of a mile, pausing every few hundred yards to examine the river. It was nowhere bigger than a trickle among ferns and stones, but it seemed cleaner, and we finally decided on a grassy hollow, well hidden by trees. There was a mealie-field between us and the trail and the trees were large, so that we had some hope of privacy, but we had scarcely dragged out the tents and begun to erect them than we saw a row of figures on the high bank opposite, squatting to watch us from a discreet distance. This was annoying but inevitable; nowhere was free from the nuisance of being spied on, and if these characters chose to sit there all day they would see nothing but the innocuous activities of the camp.

Michael's first care was to improve the water supply. The stream itself trickled from rock to rock in the depths of a leafy tunnel of palms and ferns, and by laboriously filling flour-bags with mud and sand he managed to construct a miniature dam to hold a tiny pool where one could fill a jug. This feat of engineering took several hours, which the rest of us spent in scouring around in the Land Rover, trying one direction after another for a route to take the vehicle on to the hill. We met with small success, for every trail ended in a thicket, and everywhere we went we were followed by boys. They gladly left their goats and cattle to follow us into the bush at a springy trot, whenever we stopped to negotiate some obstacle clustering closely round us with chirping cries, waiting for us to provide the next diversion. We were further worried, as we lurched through the dense tangle, by hanging festoons of that evil bean which had already caused discomfort on one occasion. Here it proliferated, twining itself invisibly through the trees and sending down showers of stinging hairs whenever our bumpy passage shook the branches. We had taken off the top of the Land Rover for greater mobility, and the poisonous fall-out, as light as disintegrated thistledown, floated into our shirts and up our nostrils. We were soon burning and scratching too much to know what we were doing, and beset as usual by boys, goats and horned cattle, finally beat a demented retreat to the camp.

Michael had completed his dam, so that water could now be fetched in modest jugfuls, and to his surprise had had a friendly visitor. This was a young native who had come wading through the grass and had greeted him by name, claiming to remember him from a visit he had once paid to Salisbury, where his brother had worked on Michael's father's farm. Michael did not remember him, but he was genuine enough, and Michael cunningly engaged him in conversation. When the usual questions had been asked and answered (we were no longer emphasizing the quest for ruins, but were usually piously following the footsteps of my father, who had been either a missionary or a White Hunter) he asked him if it were true that the Zulu people had once been known in these parts. He had been told, Michael said, by a man at the cattle-dip that this was so, but did not know whether to believe it. Yes, said the young man, that was certainly true; a Zulu chief who had been defeated by his brother had been exiled to these parts. He had brought his followers with him, mostly women, the widows of his warriors, and these women had married the local men and the chief had prospered. He had even grown rich and lived to a great age, and was buried, the young man believed, not far away. 'Oh, where?' said Michael, trying not to look interested; but this the young man said he did not know. Somewhere hereabouts; the old men would remember; somewhere not many miles from his old kraal. He did not know where the kraal had been, and Michael was chary of pressing him. He gave him a small present from our stores (cornflakes, I think; we were always trying to get rid of them) and sent him on his way apparently happy.

We pondered this incident at our evening meal, when time and cold water had soothed our burning skins and we were able to hold a coherent conversation. It was good to find our story further confirmed; we would have liked to hear the answers to more questions if we had not been always afraid of betraying interest. Would the young man repeat Michael's questions to his elders? Would they eventually reach the ears of the Portuguese police? We hoped not, for the Portuguese by this time had become bogies, and whenever we heard a sound which might have been (but never was) a jeep, we stopped talking and strained our ears to listen. We were not reassured by Michael's confident proposal that if they came we should 'surround them and take the bolts out of their rifles', for what the Portuguese police would be doing while we performed this manœuvre was never made clear,

F

and we did not share his confidence that such a *coup* would be the end of the matter, even if it were possible.

We went to bed early that night, before the little greenish-grey parrots inhabiting our trees had quite done fluttering and shrieking; they seemed disturbed by the fire, and kept up a quarrelsome racket in the high branches. At last all was quiet; the moon was rising slowly, already on the wane, and we fell asleep before it had dissolved the darkness. I do not know how long we slept in peace, gathering our energies for the morning; it was perhaps midnight when we were all awakened by a yell and I sat up in bed, my teeth chattering with shock. But it was not the Portuguese, nor any human, but only a small lemur-like animal with a long tail, a night-ape, parading the high branches over my bed. The darkness vibrated with the cry, and as soon as the silence flowed back, it did it again. It was a murderous sound, expressing the night-ape's tenderest longings of love, and so, no doubt, most melting to his kind; but to human ears it was the noise a sheeted ghost might make in a graveyard to dismay travellers; a yell of menace, the shriek of an afreet. The wretched creature repeated the performance tirelessly at intervals of about a quarter of an hour, until even Peter, who normally slept through anything, was shouting from his tent, 'For God's sake shoot the bloody thing, can't you?' and Michael was sitting up in bed with his rifle. We would all happily have seen its body drop from the trees, but it was a creature of darkness and invisible, crying its love in a secret fastness of branches, and it was not until five o'clock, in the first faint light when our chickens began to stir and crow in the dog-kennel, that I saw it run nimbly along a limb and take squirrel-leaps from tree to tree, silent at last like a ghost in flight from the morning.

Cross and unrefreshed, we set out early in the Land Rover to make a last attempt to get it up the hill. Only Michael now believed that this was possible, but he was so positive in his theory, and the advantages of success would be so great that we thought it worth spending the morning in a final effort. He was sure that if we followed the course of the river to a point where it seemed to skirt the foot of the hill, and then 'cut fifty or a hundred yards straight through the bush', we should arrive on an almost treeless and easy-looking slope, which we had all seen and longed for in the distance. The disastrous truth was, however, that on this side Nyabánga was protected by a jungle valley worse than any we had tried, and when we had hacked a course into it we sank finally into a spongy morass of reeds and thornbushes.

To get into this ridiculous position we had come down a precipitous slope where in order to make the least progress we had had to lever out boulders and fell saplings. We went on because it was even less practicable to go back. Michael, manfully slashing ahead, was badly stung by the fiendish buffalo-bean which hung in festoons in every tree and had made every inch of this swampy jungle its own. We soon saw why, in spite of the oozy richness of the soil, there were no tracks in this tangled waste, no mealie-patch, no pockets of cultivation; it was wholly subjugated by this torturous plant, which in every direction spread its invisible net. At last we saw an open space in the thicket, and Peter, who by now was driving the Land Rover like a tank, crashed headlong through a thorn-brake to reach it. He did not see that the thorn branches over his head were laden with creeper, and his violent passage precipitated such an explosion of buffalo-bean that the air became thick and golden with floating hairs. They covered the Land Rover, drifted in our nostrils, and enveloped Peter wholly as in a shower of pollen. By the time we had followed him out on to what proved to be an old mealie-patch on the far side of the thicket, he was already tearing at his arms and neck and stamping about in a fever of blasphemous misery.

It is a property of this loathsome plant (which is also, with justice, called the Nessus-bean) that nothing but time can bring its victims relief. For a hideous hour the itching and burning are acute, and scratching, which no poor wretch in his transports

can resist, raises the irritation to a mad pitch. None of us suffered
so abominably as Peter, but we were all scalded, and writhed in
grotesque contortions around the Land Rover. We tried swabbing our skins with water from our bottles and rubbed ourselves
with oil from the skins of *naartjes*, but neither brought even the
illusion of relief. We were in no state to go on, yet could not
stand still, and to an unaffected spectator the scene must have
been quite as diverting as those on the walls of some medieval
churches, with the damned writhing like maggots under demons'
pitchforks.

There were spectators, of course. The noise of our progress
through the valley must have been heard a mile off, and now that
we were through the worst of it, and had come to an open patch
to which there were paths, first boys with goats appeared and
then two young men, who watched our plight with enjoyment
from a little distance. The younger of the two was perhaps seventeen; he had a gentle face and carried a home-made zither. After
watching us for a while in silence he struck a tentative note and
then another, and eventually played a plaintive four-note tune,
as though prompted by our contortions to some accompaniment.
The other was unusually handsome, with the proud bearing and
features of the Zulu. He approached us presently with an air of
amusement, and told Michael, who was either less afflicted or
more stoical than the rest of us, and was recovering his dignity,
that nobody went into the place through which we had come
because there was an evil plant in it. Whenever they themselves
were stung they plunged into the river or covered themselves
with mud, but neither remedy was much good; one could only
bear it and wait. This we were doing to the best of our ability;
poor Peter was crimson from head to foot and looked like a man
in a fever. We were glad to ask for directions for getting out,
and the youths obligingly led us into the thicket for some way,
to a point where there was a distinguishable trail, and suddenly
left us, vanishing silently into the fronded reeds.

It was now midday, and we were still far from our hill, which appeared and reappeared mockingly at a distance, serene and bright under the vertical sun. We now knew finally that there was no way of helping ourselves with the Land Rover, and that the hill would always defeat us until we approached it on foot. The day was too far spent for another attempt, and we were in no condition to make one. We were thankful at last to reach the watering-place, and to bump our way over the difficult trail to the camp, where we washed in cold water and changed every article of clothing.

A message had come in our absence which brought Michael to a standstill, for he was always careful in matters of bush etiquette. The camp was not, as we had supposed, back in Zamchiya's territory, but on a spur of land in the jurisdiction of another chief, towards whom we had failed in courtesy by not asking his permission. The message said simply that the Chief, Chiquoqueti, had heard of the presence of strangers, and the implication was clear that we should take him a gift and pay him an apologetic visit. Peter and Jack were still only convalescent from their sufferings, so when we had eaten and rested and cautiously brushed the carpet of hairs from the Land Rover, I went on this courtesy visit alone with Michael. We were hard put to it to know what to take for a present, for we were down to our last bottle of whisky and were regretting several that had already been given away. Spirits and shot are by far the most coveted gifts, since Africans are not allowed to buy either, with tins of beer or fruit a poor second. Our beer had all been finished at the lorry festival, and most of our remaining shot was for rifles, which a chief could not possess, so we packed some tins of apricots round our feet, hoping that it was true (as we had been told) that this chief, though renowned for wisdom, was a very poor one.

We went up the stony hill above the cattle-dip and came soon enough to a small and dilapidated kraal where a very old man in khaki shorts was dozing outside his hut. This was evidently Chiquoqueti himself, for he bolted inside as soon as he saw us coming and sent out two of his sons to ask our business. Michael told me to stay where I was, in the Land Rover, since he did not wish to make matters worse by approaching the Chief with a woman, and I sat unobtrusively in the shade while he and the sons went through the conversational preliminaries. When the Chief emerged he was evidently in full dress, consisting of an army winter overcoat. It was of an obsolete pattern and almost threadbare, but the buttons had been polished to the last dazzle of perfection.

The conversation was long, and from first to last the Chief's manner was forbidding. He was not pleased to see us, and received Michael's apology in silence. He did not refuse the tins, but would not look at them, and Michael had the impression that the prime cause of his displeasure was our coming without warning, catching him off his guard in a state of undress. He was a fine-looking old man and I longed for a photograph, and this was eventually permitted, though he would neither remove his coat nor relax his disapproving and suspicious expression. We came away with the feeling that he believed not a word that had been said, and had formed an impression of us that was deeply unfavourable.

After this chilling interview we cheered ourselves by visiting the large and prosperous-looking kraal which we had once supposed to be Zamchiya's. We now knew that it belonged to my old friend of the pink woollen cap; he had come to the camp while we were on the hill, and had left a request for four gallons of petrol. We had not much to spare, but we needed fresh meat and a couple of *pangas*, since both of ours had been lost by Shorty on wood-cutting forays, and this seemed an opportunity for bargaining. Our friend was a man of importance, by African standards a highly prosperous farmer: he had twelve wives and fifty-six children, and himself never needed to raise a finger.

He came out expansively to meet us, snatching off his woollen cap and holding it with ringed hands against his breast. The women and children dawdling about the huts, each one languidly occupied in some unexacting task, fetching water, stirring a pot, shooing chickens, backed respectfully away at his approach, keeping out of range of the eye of authority. One of the younger women was hugely pregnant, and walked with the backward-sloping gait of the precariously balanced. Others had babies bulging from a cotton satchel; most of them had naked children at their heels. One was the fat young woman who had talked to me so effusively at the cattle-dip, but in her husband's presence she neither raised her eyes nor returned my greeting. The kraal was tidily kept and had an air of discipline; everything in it reflected the personality of the master. He radiated natural authority, and that innocent charm that one encounters only in those who have never had a moment's doubt of being in the right. Maside (for that was his name) was delighted to be visited, and even seemed not to mind that one of his guests was of the despised sex; he made special remarks to Michael for my benefit, and as they were translated watched my face with an expression of eager vanity and politeness. It now transpired that his approaching me on the day that I had been waiting on the ant-hill had been due to a belief that I was lost, and a desire to offer help and hospitality. I thanked him through Michael, and he shook his head, laughing. It was nothing, he said; I had seemed to be alone, and this was difficult country.

He showed us his cattle with great pride; there were rather too many of them, but they were in fair condition. He should have more, he said, but wives were dear in these parts and his family had impoverished him. For some, he said, opening his eyes wide, he had paid the equivalent in cattle of fifty pounds. He began pointing out his wives to us as he spoke, quoting the price of each as a measure of the cost of modern living. Michael, running a disparaging eye over the group, suggested that he had paid too much for some of them, and with this disobliging remark Maside agreed. It could not be helped, he said; things were exorbitant.

He showed a strong bargaining vein when it came to business, laughing and shaking his head at Michael's suggestions and making impudent calculations on his fingers. But the performance was largely for pleasure; he sold us a goat for a pound, which was about right, and went up to a kid and two *pangas* for four gallons of petrol. On this he had perhaps the better bargain, for petrol was not to be got within fifty miles; but having displayed cunning he showed an oriental desire to appease us with presents. He sent a girl into one of the huts for a handsome calabash and placed it in my hands; it was new and unused, of a capacity of about four quarts. Then he shouted a command to the fat wife, who obediently crawled into the pigeon-house, and emerged again backwards after an anxious struggle, holding a large beaky black-and-white fledgling. She approached slowly, eyes cast down, tenderly carrying the bird like a precious vessel, and knelt to offer it up to her husband's hands. He placed it at once in mine with a gallant speech; apparently Michael had told him it was my birthday.

The pigeon was quiet and did not seem to mind handling, but we were next invited to climb up a ladder of branches to inspect the corn-loft, which was a thatched barn on legs, eight feet from the ground; and with the bird in my hands I found the ascent difficult. The floor of the barn was woven of springy branches, and the cobs of maize were stacked in rows to the roof, as orderly and beautiful to look at as a well-stocked library. Maside had already sold his surplus at a good price, and what we saw now was the coming year's supply, enough to feed his numerous wives and children.

Not all the family was at home at this time: the grown-up sons were mostly absent, working for the Portuguese, and some of the daughters had been disposed of in marriage; but the population of the kraal was still impressive, and the wives in their dark kilts and bright beads were, though a homely lot, pleasing. I asked permission to photograph the family, and this was received with pleasure by our host. He clapped his hands and gave a brief command, and they all disappeared at once into their separate huts. They were gone for a long time, while I chose a spot and set my camera and Michael talked to Maside and fondled the pigeon. When they finally emerged it was evident that they had gone to immense trouble and had ruined their appearance. Each was dressed in a hideous and ill-fitting cotton frock, of the deplorable kind that hangs in bunches at the back of every kaffir store in Africa. I had often examined these when we had had occasion to go into a store for bully-beef or paraffin, and had been appalled at the shoddy material and crass workmanship supplied to Africans; the two handkerchiefs I had bought of the same cotton had run their bright colours into a sorry mess at the first touch of water, and I had been relieved when Hla-Hla told me they were not Lancashire goods, but had been manufactured in Rhodesia.

The wives now ranged themselves with their children under Maside's orders, the few sons who were at home standing in a row on either side of their father. A Portuguese felt hat was brought for Maside and the family's finery was complete. Every vestige of beauty was blotted out from the group, and I knew that I had taken a grotesque picture. The taking of it, however, was received as a compliment, and we parted from Maside on excellent terms. It did not strike us until later that it was odd he had not asked us what we were doing; indeed he had not put to us any of the usual questions.

The following morning we left camp early, taking food and water and leaving the Land Rover under the trees at the watering-place. We followed Jack's route, which he had marked with knotted grasses and bent twigs, and got to the top of the hill in under two hours, having lost ourselves only twice. It was a still day with pockets of mist in the hollows; the grass was moist and untrodden, cold with dew. There seemed to be nobody about, not even herd-boys, and the silence, though reassuring, was oppressive. We were all uncomfortably conscious of the shortness of time, for in two days Michael's extended leave would be up, and we were painfully on the alert for the Portuguese Commissioner. It was strange that we had been left in peace for so long, but we knew that this was only a matter of time, and that when we returned to camp he might be there before us. So long as we had left no mark on the hill and had not begun to dig, there was no reason why we should not stick to our cover-story, which though eccentric was harmless; but once we had begun tunnelling the pretence would collapse, and we would have to work fast and get out quickly. Many considerations pointed to these two days being the last we could spend on the hill, for our repeated climbing was constantly watched, as our own Africans, who gossiped at the cattle-dip, had already reported; they themselves were openly uneasy about it, and their recent questions had driven Michael to invent improbabilities.

We made up our minds, since these last two days were all that were left us, to devote the whole of the first to searching the hill, in particular to examining the mound with the big tree. If we found nothing to disturb our guess that the mound was what we were looking for, we could cut a trench into the side on the second day, and make new plans according to what we discovered. If this misty silence continued, it might augur well; we might, if need be, be able to work through the night, and if the Portuguese police arrived at the camp they would not find their way up the hill in a hurry. At all events, and if the hill yielded nothing, we would still have to leave the area as quickly as possible. Our clues ended here. Nyabánga was the end of the trail that had defeated Russell.

Arrived at last breathless and sweating at the wood-cutters' shelter, we stretched ourselves on the hard ground and watched the last tendrils of mist dissolve from the hill. The blood was beating in our ears and we did not speak; but after a heavy-breathing silence first one of us sat up and then another; it was not our hearts making the whole rhythm. Somewhere below the hill we could hear a drum.

We had not heard a drum of any sort since we had crossed the border, and the beat we now felt rather than heard, tentative and muffled as though speaking with deliberate discretion, was quite different from the cheerful drumming of the beer-drinking.

It began with heavy, slow, portentous thuds, which after a pause went into a light irregular staccato passage, followed by silence. After an interval which seemed endless but was really about a quarter of an hour, the heavy drum spoke again, and the light passage was repeated. 'They're sending a message,' said Michael.

We listened with apprehension, watching his face, but he could not read the drums, and shook his head. All he could distinguish after the third passage was that the same message was being repeated, and presently it was taken up at a distance, by another drum on the farther side of the hill. The heavy beats were simply an alert, an announcement that a message was being sent, and the second drum had received it and was passing it on. It might have nothing to do with us, but in the still air the distant thudding had a tone of menace, urgent, yet deliberately covert.

Startled out of fatigue, we scrambled to our feet. Whatever the meaning of the drums there was no time to be lost, and we hurriedly separated to quarter the hill. My way was across the top to the north face, and after studying the tops of such trees as I thought I should recognize, I plunged into the grass. Again I had the sensation of walking under water, through a heavy forest of weed that closed over my head. As far as I could judge, pausing occasionally to look upwards to the surface, the grass in places was nearly ten feet high, and there seemed little hope of ever seeing out of it. At the level at which I forced a laborious passage it was laced together with the débris of past seasons, and the matted stuff dragged hard against my thighs. It was difficult to cut and I dragged it apart with my hands, pausing at each step for further unravelling. The trail I made was a narrow corridor, which at last I should be able to retrace, but it was futile to imagine that much of the hill could be examined by this method, unless one pursued it for days, making a maze of ant-like runs over the whole surface. By the time I reached the north side the sun was blazing vertically down out of a white sky and seed-pods were cracking open in the heat with a papery rattle. The grass was less dense here and I could see out of it in places, but nowhere was there a sign of a trail, a mound, or of anyone having passed this way for years. I took scraps of paper out of my pockets and impaled them on thorns as I went along, marking my passage, and they hung there motionless and ridiculous, like fragments lodged in the weed at the bottom of the sea.

We were out of sight of one another for perhaps two hours, and all this time the drums murmured their monotonous tattoo. Sometimes the sound was screened by a fold of the hill, and I could hear nothing but the dry rustle of my own progress; but sooner or later the old vibration would assert itself and I would catch a faint beat from a new position. This continual losing and finding of the sound was a disturbing sensation, as though one were hiding and being repeatedly discovered, and in the end my ears grew so weary of listening to the drums that I could not tell if I were hearing them or not.

At last I heard the distant shrilling of a police whistle, the signal we had agreed on for returning, and made my way back through my grassy catacombs to the first meeting-place. The others had covered far more ground than I had, my area having been even denser than theirs, and they had found nothing to compare with the mound with the big tree. The species of tree they had not been able to identify; they had not seen one like it before, and it was the only one of its kind to be found on the hill. It was an evergreen, not unlike an ilex, with small hard dark-green leaves which when broken gave off an aromatic smell. It was growing out of the top of a fair-sized mound, and from its central position appeared to have been planted. The place was thickly surrounded and overgrown, and except for the openings in the grass that had been made that morning there was no sign of any trail or visitation. All this was suggestive enough in a place where we had found no other mound, not even an ant-hill, but there were other curious features which seemed significant. This tree, the biggest on the hill, could be seen for miles; it was Nyabánga's only distinguishable mark, and we had seen it from as far away as M'jenami. The mound itself was a little below the crown of the hill, facing across the plain to Umzila's country. It was the only spot on the hill where, without climbing or lifting oneself in any way, one looked over an open sweep of forest and bush, leading the eye straight to a gap in the far hills, beyond which lay the shadowy curve of the M'rongwezi. It was thus the only place on Nyabánga from which one looked straight as an arrow into Umzila's country, to the very river on which he had built his kraal. It also—and this again seemed to be more than chance—was the sole point from which the western edge of M'jenami was seen in coincidence with the outline of a sister mountain, M'jervasi, the two standing like fortresses on the fringe of Umzila's country, enclosing it to the south-west in a rocky frame. If Umzila's grave were indeed on Nyabánga, it was from here alone that his spirit's eye could gaze on its old home; and here the mound was raised, crowned with its tree.

We stood there for a long time, gazing at the writhen roots and the hardness of the mound under our feet, suddenly aware of the task that lay before us. There was no longer any doubt in our minds that this was the place, and we probed in imagination into the stony ground, splintering the tree-roots, tunnelling the clay, to the dark cavity we could almost see, the sense of it was so powerful. It was a forbidding obstacle, and the atmosphere of the place—our imaginations were no doubt at work, but who knows?—intimidating. Under our feet, perhaps six feet down, perhaps more, a skull might be gazing upwards from empty sockets, unmoved after seventy years of that rich darkness, secure in the age-old protection of fear and magic. What business had we to disturb him? None, we knew; yet all four stood rooted to the mound, staring downwards, as though our feet were held by an invisible magnet. When at last we broke away, closing the divided grasses to cover our tracks, we became dimly aware of the drums again, monotonously muttering, and woke out of our dream to consider present problems. We would dig the mound tomorrow, drums or no drums, and prepare a speedy retreat from Umzila's country.

We met no one, not even a child or a goat, on the way down; except for the drums, which spoke always at a distance, the bush was unusually quiet. We followed one another in single file and in silence, through the maze of hair-like paths which at last, after so many errors, we were beginning to learn, and came to the watering-place a good hour before sunset, to find the Land Rover surrounded by thirsty cattle. This was the hour when the herd-boys brought them in droves to the muddy shallows, from miles of burnt-up bush where there was no juice in the grass and the stream-beds were all dry; a convivial hour which the youths enlivened with simple showing-off, with walking on their hands and tinkling and blowing on their musical instruments. We had watched them often, laughing at their antics which were sometimes aimed at us as a heaven-sent audience; but this evening they were quiet and seemed to avoid us, watching in sombre groups from the slimy bank.

As we rocked our way over the bumps of the homeward journey we discussed all possible tactics for the morrow. The ideal thing from a practical point of view would have been to take John and Shorty with us, since five men dig faster and farther than three, and they were both of them strong and skilled with pick and shovel. But it was too great a risk. Used as they were to Michael's authority, there was no knowing how the fit would take them when they realized (as they eventually must) what we were doing, and Michael shook his head at the suggestion. No white man's order, he said, would weigh in the balance against superstition, and we should be fools indeed if we risked their running away and telling some garbled story in the villages. They had already asked too many questions for his liking, and the stories he had told them had been so far on the safe side of truth that it was better not to disturb them. We would leave the boys busy with packing up the camp, and would be as secret as possible with the digging equipment.

This was another difficulty. We had little enough in the way of digging tools, and did not wish to be seen with them on the hill. The heads of the mattock and pick could be taken off their shafts and hidden in knapsacks, with the handles carried as sticks or strapped to the rifles; but the spade was so constructed that it could not be dismembered, and defied every attempt at ingenuity. We examined it carefully that night, but it was obvious that once we took it apart we should never reassemble it; it had got to be carried whole or it would be useless. It was decided at last that the thing should be wrapped in a blanket and carried in a bandolier. So disguised it presented a curious appearance, not unlike a large and ungainly banjo, and was hidden under some sacking in the Land Rover. The *pangas* were normal equipment and could be carried openly, but when everything had been put together for the morning—tool-heads in knapsacks, rifles, *pangas*, water-bottles, cameras (we were always supposed to be keenly photographing scenery)—we were appalled to find them so heavy. We took out the tin of bully-beef and coffee, resolved to make do with water and a handful of biscuits, and I rejected the heavy snake-bite outfit which I had so far painstakingly carried over every inch of ground, haunted by the idea that once I abandoned it somebody was certain to be bitten; but these minor adjustments made no appreciable difference, and we sighed to think what we should sweat under tomorrow.

All the time we had been busy with the tools, John had been lurking in and out of the shadows, waiting for an opportunity of speaking to Michael. What he wanted was a *squeret*, or advance on his wages; he needed, he said, a pound. This would not have been unusual in a place that offered the means of spending money, but here, with no store within miles and no meeting-place beyond the deserted cattle-dip, it seemed peculiar, and Michael asked the reason. 'Sorry, Boss, can't say.' John was respectful but firm, and all Michael's questioning and cajolery failed to move him. 'All right,' said Michael, 'I shan't let you be a fool with your money unless you tell me what it's for,' and stalked off to his tent with a displeased expression, quite sure that John, who was a confiding character, would presently follow him. But he did not; and when Michael came out of the tent again he saw John slipping unobtrusively out of the camp with a bundle. He brought him up with a shout, and John came reluctantly into the firelight with his hands behind him. He had been on his way to the cattle-dip to sell his clothes.

'What the hell are you going to do that for? They're your best ones, aren't they?'

'Yes, Boss. I need that pound.'

'Tell me what you want it for and I'll give you the pound now.'

'Very sorry, Boss. No.' And the tedious argument was gone through all over again, with John respectful, apologetic, immovable.

A pound was a serious proportion of his weekly wages, which according to custom would be paid in a lump when we returned to Salisbury, and Michael was afraid that he had got into some silly trouble with the local inhabitants, or was being swindled. But it was no use. John meant to have that pound, and would not say why, and after a further struggle Michael gave it to him.

We had hardly settled round the fire for a drink, remarking with relief that the drums were at last silent, when the cook appeared and asked for an advance. He, too, wanted a pound, and the only reason he would give was that it was 'for something important'. Michael was adamant, but Jack produced the money out of his pocket; it hardly seemed worth while at this stage having trouble with the cook. When Shorty, however, appeared with a wheedling expression, cap in hand, hair meekly parted down the middle, asking for a pound, Michael's impatience exploded, and he took Shorty behind the lorry for questioning, which he did by the simple expedient of offering to kick him. This practical technique of persuasion was only too familiar, and Shorty gave in. If Boss Michael would kindly refrain from telling the others, he should know the story.

It now leaked out that while we had been on the hill the local witch-doctor had sent a confidential message to our Africans. Since they were strangers, he said, he wished to do them a kindness, and would allow them to buy, for a pound a bottle, a secret and powerful medicine. The valuable property of this medicine was, that wherever the owner of it happened to be, it would make him aware of any danger that threatened him. Complete protection lay in the bottle itself, for even against an intending murderer one teaspoonful of the medicine was effective. Conveniently enough, it was the victim and not the murderer who took the dose; the magic made him immune from every harm. There were two footnotes, so to speak, to this information. One was, that the witch-doctor would not like to say that this was a safe area, where harm was never done to unwelcome strangers. The other concerned the medicine, which as well as beneficent had malignant properties. If any man to whom it was offered refused to buy it, for instance, it would attack him; wherever he was in the world, in whatever company, its baneful influence would follow and overtake him.

Michael had seen quite enough in his lifetime of the effects of magic to know that argument was useless. John's Christianity, the cook's sophistication, even Shorty's allegiance to the Dutch Reformed Church would avail them nothing. They were possessed of the virgin faith which moves mountains, and the witch-doctor (by now, no doubt, filling his little bottles with muddy water) had the formula for setting it in motion. He said every blasphemous thing he could think of about the witch-doctor, making Shorty's eyes revolve with anxious terror, and came back to the fire with the news that he had given him the money. We would have 'scoff' early that night, to leave the boys free to visit the witch-doctor and purchase their immunity from evil. They might need it, he said soberly, before we got out from here. It would be nice if we ourselves could have had a bottle.

This idea seemed to the rest of us worth pursuing, but apparently it was out of the question. Witch-doctors kept prudently clear of Europeans, and were rarely seen by them. They enjoyed a power equal if not superior to that of the chiefs, did considerable good as faith-healers among their own people, and could hardly be blamed if they ran a few profitable rackets. Wasn't it the same, Michael reasonably said, in Harley Street? We considered this carefully over our whisky and had to admit that, given a public as pure in heart as the witch-doctor's and as innocent of doubt, there were no lengths to which a skilful practitioner might not go. The simplicity of the idea was almost beautiful.

Still, there were aspects of it which were not reassuring. Had the witch-doctor thought it out for himself, or was there something afoot which had suggested this brilliant and profitable sideline? From what, tomorrow perhaps, would the medicine protect them? From the Portuguese, or the wrath of Umzila's spirit? This was a disagreeable line of thought, and we had not pursued it long in the dying firelight when once more, at no great distance, the drums began.

The pattern, so far as we could judge, was the same as before: heavy booming thumps at regular intervals, followed by silence, followed by the light rapid complex staccato message. We strained our ears to listen, and after the second or third repeat heard a muffled answer a long way off, like an echo, and then the two seemed to speak at the same time, to overlap in muttering counterpoint and to fall silent together. After a time we could not tell if there were one or two drums conversing, or even three; the far one was so faint that we might have imagined it; in the silence an ominous pulse beat in one's ears.

With the boys gone, the camp was dark and quiet; we had nothing more to say and went to bed. The drums continued to beat alone until midnight, coming up from the pillow more as sensation than sound, so that one constantly raised one's head for a moment to listen; and at midnight the night-ape loosed his opening yell, adding his banshee voice to the concerto. We slept fitfully, waking to the night-ape's screams and to sudden silences, and at three o'clock to the boys' return, which was drunken and noisy. The final silence was a long time coming. When at last it fell the little doves were beginning and the first grey light was prefacing the morning.

10

The Dig

THE dawn was cold; a milky river of mist had flowed into the valley and was slowly weaving tributaries round the hill. The summit was hidden; trees and grass were heavy with chilly dew. Maside's kraal and the watering-place were deserted; it was as though all life and sound had been drained away, and we moved in a world which we alone inhabited. Our packs were heavy and we climbed in silence, checking the knots of grass, the bent twigs, the private arrangements of sticks and stones which were our landmarks, and which led us faithfully through our complex channels. None of our signs, so far as we could see, had been moved, but here and there, where we changed direction or left one gully for another, there were strange ones beside the path, which we had not made. Handfuls of grass had been knotted together, forming a standing figure suggesting a totem, with a style and flourish which was none of ours. Some were mere knottings, others were like a grassy sketch of a corn-dolly; it was clear that someone had followed the trail since we had, and at key points had left mysterious signals.

We reached the top in an hour and a half, and sat for a moment to rest by the wood-cutters' shelter. It was past nine o'clock, the sun still invisible; our shirts were wet with sweat and the cold dew. There was no movement in the air and no sound anywhere; none of those small noises, cries of herd-boys, voices of women at the water, which normally floated up to the top of the hill; even the drums were silent, as though the glacier of mist had been a river indeed, spreading a chill of silence along the valley.

There was no sign that anyone had followed our trail from the summit to the mound; there were no knots or symbols here, and Shadow went before us with drooping tail, making distasteful leaps through the wet grass. The mound itself was undisturbed, the grass as we had left it; however closely our movements had been followed and our route marked, this final place at least had been avoided.

The point at which it seemed best to open a trench was on the lower side of the mound, facing downhill. By tunnelling here on the level and going straight in, we hoped to get to the centre at a depth of eight feet, using the slope of the hill to our advantage. We spoke as though we knew exactly how to do it, but I suspect none of us, except perhaps Peter on his farm, had ever tried to dig a trench in his life, and we thought enviously of Russell's mining experience. He and his confederates had trenched and cross-trenched the whole of Umzila's kraal, which years of use would have beaten to rocky hardness, with the floors of the old huts as durable as cement. We were faced with a mound which had never been trodden, which only time and the tree had together fortified; but at the first blow of the pick we exchanged glances; the mound was as hard and as strong as a stone sepulchre.

It was decided that the three men should take turns at the digging, working in twenty-minute shifts, one digging, one resting, and one shovelling. Shadow and I were deputed to keep watch, since in the silence and the mist it would have been easy for spies to approach from any quarter, and what share we might have taken in the digging (we were both willing) could have been nothing but a nuisance. We spoke in whispers, aware that in this still and moisture-laden air the least sound carried to a distance; but as soon as digging began precaution was useless; the blows of the pick could have been heard a mile off. Shadow and I set off on our cautious rounds and I climbed a shaky tree which served as a lookout; but nothing stirred, and we heard nothing but the thud of the pick and the pebbly scrabble of shovelling. The mist was dispersing slowly, growing pearly and luminous under the diffused sun; vapour drifted out of the trees in shreds; it would soon be hot.

The surface of the mound was cement-hard and had been worked by ants, which was alarming, for although no other ant-hills had been seen it was always possible that this was a solitary citadel; we had seen many as large in other parts of the country. The galleries were old, however, and after a few inches they disappeared and the pick broke out impacted clay and pebbles. The trench went in between two major tree-roots, which held the mound in a vice of knotted arms, but when it was two feet deep and about four feet long more roots appeared, driven down-wards through the clay like a portcullis. These were attacked and splintered with mattock and *pangas* and levered out in pieces with the crowbar, Michael and Peter throwing out the débris between their legs like dogs and Jack clearing the earth with a shovel be-hind them. We were still too near the outer surface of the mound to be examining the refuse with great attention, but an unfamiliar sound on the spade made Jack pause, and probe in the loose earth that he had just thrown. There was something there all right, a fine potsherd, curved and smooth as on the day it was fired.

The others came out of the trench and we all examined it, passing it from hand to hand in speechless excitement. It was a piece of a native pot, and the curve suggested that it had not been a large one. It would have been natural to find such a fragment if we had been digging a hut, but here, three feet below the surface of this uninhabited hill, how could it be other than sig-nificant? The three signs of a grave that Russell had repeatedly sought for had been a mound, a tree, and (as evidence of occa-sional pious observances) a beer-pot. The mound and the tree were all that we had had so far, and the potsherd seemed like magical confirmation. From the curve, we judged it too small to have been a water-pot, and there was, besides, no water on

Nyabánga. This steep dry summit was in the highest degree unlikely ever to have been inhabited. Why then should a pot have
been left or broken here? Could it not have been one of the
beer-pots that Russell had mentioned, placed on the mound
years ago for the old man's spirit? Umzila had been dead about
seventy years, too long for there to be any likelihood of recent
observances, but twenty or thirty years ago perhaps, before the
roots and débris of thirty seasons had added to the mound or the
ants carried their structures over the pyramid, the surface would
have been lower, and at the level from which the spade had
thrown up the shard a pot of beer might well have been set in the
grass.

We returned to the trench and sifted the earth with our hands,
and in the trodden floor, as well as in the loose earth thrown
away at random, found several more fragments. They were all
of the same thickness and colour and belonged presumably to the
same vessel, but too much was broken and lost to reconstruct it,
and since the edges were all of the same colour as the surface we
could not tell whether the pot had been broken that morning by
the pick, or had lain for many years in separate fragments.

The detail was not important; the fragments themselves were
food to the imagination, and the diggers returned to their work
with fierce energy. In the course of another hour the trench was
deepened, so that even Michael was hidden to the shoulders, the
pick flashing regularly upward into the sunlight and thudding
down into the hard clay so that the leaves trembled. It was killing
work: after twenty minutes each crawled out of the trench and
lay sweating and speechless on the grass, glad to relax his aching
muscles until another shift was gone and he must begin shovelling. We were all thirsty, the men from labour and I from anxiety
and suspense; when the heat of noon was on us we had emptied
our water-bottles. We were all by this time subject to a strange
ebbing and flowing of illusion, as though our eyes had moments
of abnormal vision and could see through stones and earth to the
mound's centre. At such times the mind's eye pierced clear

through the barrier of earth to the inner chamber, where Umzila's bones lay couched in their airless burrow, already shaken by
the tremors of our assault. The men dug like demons, believing
at such moments that each next blow would open a crumbling
hole into the final cavity, and that we should fall on the dark
mouth with crowbar and mattock.

But this hallucinated state was not constant. As blow after
blow dislodged always harder earth, or bit with a jarring shock
into iron-hard roots, fatigue and despair would blot out the
inner vision, imposing instead a conviction of solid rock and
earth, impacted without a crevice to the hill's foundations.

As the hours passed, and the hardness of the earth increased
with the pains of fatigue, this hopeless vision became more frequent; the difficulties of the trench were now so extreme, allow-
ing no room to turn or swing the pick sideways, that it finally
became obvious that it would have to be widened before we
could go farther. Michael climbed out of the trench, complaining
of pain in his shoulders, and Peter, who had been wrapping
pieces of rag round his blistered hands, went in with the mattock
to widen the head of the trench. He had not been at it many
minutes when a chopping blow dislodged a fall of earth, revealing
what looked like a fragment of stone wall. He gave a shout, and
we crowded over the edge of the trench to see. He was scraping
with the head of the mattock at what appeared to be a vertical
surface of old brickwork, or rather a dark-coloured dry-stone
wall laid in regular courses, smaller and smoother than those we
had seen in Masingo, but not dissimilar.

Our hopes soared once more, and the next hour was spent in
heavy digging and shovelling at the head of the trench, in an
effort to widen it sufficiently to uncover the wall. The trench
had now penetrated well in towards the centre of the mound on a
downward slope, and at the head was partly roofed in by the
roots of the tree. We had arrived at a point where, if stonework
existed to sustain and protect a cavity, this was about where one
would expect to find it; we could not be more than a couple of

yards from the centre. It seemed impossible to dislodge the stones without having more room to move, but time was slipping away and the tree-roots buttressed the trench like iron stanchions. Sweating and exasperated, but sure like the rest of us that his blows sounded hollow, Peter attacked the face of the wall with extra fury, smashing some stones and breaking the shaft of the mattock.

This was a disaster, but we still had the pick and the crowbar, and were too much excited to care. The end of the crowbar was thrust at a downward angle into one of the crevices, and the three men brought their combined weight to bear. At this moment Shadow, who had wandered off unnoticed into the bushes, suddenly barked, and I sprang up in panic, guiltily aware that the watch had been forgotten. I could not find him at first, and searched anxiously through the grass in several directions. The men were so intent on their levering that they had not heard him, and I was on the point of going back to raise the alarm when I heard the rustle and thud of Shadow pouncing, and in the shaking grass found him gaily absorbed in the pursuit of some small animal. This was a dereliction of duty and shook me badly; he had been left on guard by Michael at the back of the mound, and was as bad as I was. Who might not have crept up unseen while I lay face downwards, staring into the trench, and Shadow deserted his post in enormous boredom? I called him sharply to me and returned to the mound, to find the men standing back from a heap of rubble. They had levered the wall apart and could see what it was: no wall at all but a freak accretion of clays. It now lay in shattered débris at their feet, disclosing rock which not even the tree had fissured. Could it be that this earth had been undisturbed for centuries?

At this we sat down on the edge of the trench in silence, and presently said what was uppermost in our minds. Strangely enough, it was not that we felt we had followed a blind alley. I believe the magnetic sensation of being on the very roof of Umzila's chamber was stronger in all of us at that moment than at any other time, and the taste in our mouths was the bitter taste of frustration. Our tools were inadequate, that was the first admission; and the second was that we needed more time and more men. 'If we had five or six *munts*,' said Michael, 'and worked in shifts, we could tunnel right into the bloody thing in a day.'

'Not with these tools,' said Peter; 'look at the mattock. What we need is an experienced miner and a charge of dynamite.' Jack glanced at the rock and said nothing; I guessed he was thinking of Russell.

'If we could come back later,' said Michael, 'with the right stuff, and a team of *munts* for digging, and a power drill . . .' Nobody replied; we knew the answer to that. 'The hell of it is,' he concluded, 'I shall have to start for Salisbury in the morning.'

'We shall all have to start,' said Jack. 'If three of us can't do it, what chance have two?' We relapsed into silence, thinking of the week lost with the lorry in the river, and the night-long drumming, and the Portuguese Commissioner.

'How long do you give it,' said Peter at length, 'before the local gentry come up and examine the hill?' He was rewrapping the sodden bandages on his hands, and looked exhausted. We gazed at the devastation, and our hearts sank.

'I think we ought to cover it in,' said Jack, but even as he got stiffly to his feet and stooped for the shovel he knew it was hopeless. Tons of soil from the trench had been shovelled downhill, and lay spread in trampled heaps over a wide area. The mound itself was hideously cloven, tree-roots had been cut and thrown aside, branches broken, the grass hopelessly trampled. There was no concealing what we had been about, and as soon as we were off the hill we knew the word would go out that we had been digging. If, as we were still strongly inclined to believe, we had found Umzila's grave and were even now within a few feet of the treasure, our situation would be perilous. If we were wrong, the fact of our digging at all would be highly suspect, and we would be wise to get out at once, without waiting for questioning by either the local chiefs or the Native Commissioner.

Our best hope was, since the sun was already low, that no one would care to go on the hill after dark, and that our activities would not be discovered before morning. By that time we would already be breaking camp, and would be over the Rhodesian border in a few hours. As it was, we should have to move quickly; we were dismayed to find it was five o'clock and that there was only an hour of daylight. We had no wish to add to our misfortunes by losing ourselves on the hill.

We gathered our tools hastily together, having given up all idea of covering our traces, and set off without loss of time for the downward trail. The men were numb with fatigue and often stumbled, and I was too heavily burdened to be able to speak. We slipped and scrambled down through grass and thorn, searching for our private signs as the light failed, thanking Heaven we had thought to bring pocket torches. We saw no one. It was dark before we reached the area where we had left the Land Rover, and our wavering beams anxiously raked the bushes. It was there at last, hidden and safe under its screen of leaves, and we fell into it with relief. We would have been glad to move without headlights but this was impossible; in the moonless dark the noise and glare of our passage seemed outrageous.

We could not hope to return to camp unseen, but it was a shock when, in the moment of catching a glimpse of our own fire, a drum began to beat like a sudden signal. We lurched into camp and switched off the engine to listen. It sounded much nearer than before, and seemed to come from Chiquoqueti's kraal. This time there was no staccato message, only the heavy rhythmic monotonous beat, pulsing away in the dark between brief pauses.

Our boys had been watching for us, and seemed disturbed. They were plainly relieved when they heard we were leaving in the morning, and set about packing their gear by lantern-light. Shorty, Michael discovered, had already finished his bottle of magic medicine. It was obvious they did not like the drums, but would not comment on them. Michael had asked them the night before if they could interpret them, and they had said they could not; all that they claimed to know was that it was not a beer-drinking.

We were all depressed by the final admission of failure, and this ominous drumming was the last straw. We washed by candlelight and packed our clothes, all of us jumpy and more or less exhausted. It was useless to tell oneself that the drumming might have nothing to do with us; our nerves thought otherwise, and we all remembered Michael's stories of the disturbers of graves whose limbs the natives had hung like joints from the trees. We were on edge, and I came very near to frenzy when Michael in the goodness of his heart decided to cheer me up with a sprightly joke. He ran the Land Rover across the mealie-field in the dark, causing us all to stop in our packing and listen, and then lifted the flap of my tent and in an urgent voice announced the Portuguese Commissioner. I pulled on my shirt in horror, calling to Jack and Peter, and rushed out into the darkness with a torch to find Michael benignly smiling at the success of his jest. The relief of finding it was not true was so great that my eyes filled with tears, and it was some little time before I could laugh appreciatively.

But this fourth-form joke did something for us after all, for it broke the tension and made us all confess a craven relief. There were compensations in not having our pockets stuffed with diamonds, and I felt a thankfulness that surprised me. Now that all was over except departure, I knew how unequal I should have been to the fears and strains which must have followed success. I am a bad smuggler: excitement suffocates me. Conscience is a treacherous thing, and mine behaves badly whenever there is serious danger of being found out. I should have loved the diamonds, but could have wept with relief to know that I had not to fly after all to Antwerp, perhaps alone, and get them through the Customs.

Our last evening together in camp was emotional. The drums went on, sometimes near at hand and sometimes far, and although they worried us we confessed to one another that we should have felt a thousand times worse if the diamonds had been hidden that night in one of the tents. It was maddening to have failed, but there was also a cowardly comfort in not being guilty. At least, this was what we told ourselves, stretching our aching legs before the fire and circulating the last bottle of whisky. It is easy to deceive oneself in the face of failure.

'I wonder though,' said Michael, after a long silence, 'if we couldn't come back in a month or two, before the rains. With dynamite, I mean, and a miner's drill. I don't like to think of all that stuff lying buried up there for ever, doing no good to anybody.'

'What would you do if you found it?' We had discussed all this before, but the subject never palled. We all had stealthy plans for living in luxury.

'Well, first I should leave the police. Not until we had got the diamonds out, of course. I'd probably be the best one to fly them out of Africa. On my police pass, naturally. We could all meet afterwards to divide the loot, somewhere in Europe.'

We protested chivalrously that this would not be fair. Things went ill with policemen found heavy with swag; the risk would be greater for him than for a civilian.

'Well, what about you?' he said, nodding to Jack. 'It wouldn't be a nice thing for you to be caught, now would it? Think of the publicity.'

'The thing,' said Peter, 'is not to be caught at all. I don't believe anyone would suspect Jack. He looks so respectable.' They all three, I thought, looked as disreputable as one could wish; Jack and Peter had not shaved for days, and Michael for more than a month. All our clothes were torn and dilapidated and Peter had lost most of his buttons, so that his stomach was exposed. Still, there was yet time; we should have had a chance to clean ourselves in Salisbury.

'You could come to Europe later,' Jack said to Michael, 'when we'd all lain low for a while, and made the right contacts for disposing of the stones. Having left the police, of course; I may be wrong, but I think that would be advisable.'

'Would you dispose of them *all*?' I asked. 'Couldn't I keep just one? Not having it cut, you know, that mightn't be safe; but I should like to keep one medium-sized one, in a soft leather bag. It could be regarded as an investment?'

'I don't see why she shouldn't have it properly cut,' said Michael kindly. 'An uncut diamond looks like an old pebble.'

We sighed to think of the calabash of pebbles, but it was a comfortable sigh, soothed by fatigue and whisky and the heat of the fire. The drums were still muttering, and it was growing chilly.

'Of course,' said Peter, 'one of the most satisfying things of all would be to do something for Zamchiya. Not a handful of diamonds, perhaps, that would be dangerous, and I dare say he wouldn't accept them. But a nice account opened in Salisbury for his sons' education? Do you think he'd accept a bequest from some rich Europeans?'

'It would depend, I think,' said Jack, 'on whether he suspected the source of their generosity. I would imagine a chief has to be pretty careful.'

'He'll suspect all right,' said Michael, 'as soon as he hears of that bloody great hole on the hill. And so will everybody else. I should like to be a fly on the wall in the D.C.'s office when the news gets to Spungabera.'

But I was already concocting an explanation of the hole, for though I did not care what Chiquoqueti thought, or the local inhabitants, or the Portuguese for that matter, the thing that lay heavily on my mind was the kindness of Zamchiya. In a lesser degree I was uneasy about the missionaries, for they were the sort of people who would be shocked by expedient lies, and we had told them plenty. I was determined that when we were over the border we should visit them both, and tell them one more ameliorating lie to make my conscience comfortable. We would of course have been pursuing our search for ruins on Nyabánga, and having finally seen a mound that suggested earthworks, have carried out a little exploratory dig. We would unfortunately have found nothing but a few potsherds, which we could innocently show them. On Nyabánga, we would say, we had drawn a blank, but we were sure there were ruins to be found in this part of Africa. It is best to leave behind an impression of probity.

That night we slept lightly, for the drums continued as long as darkness lasted. We were up before sunrise, snatching a hasty breakfast while the tents sagged and came down, while beds were stripped and dismembered and boxes piled in confusion into the lorry. We had expected to wake dejected, sour over the failure of our adventure, but instead were buoyed up on a wave of absurd elation. Nothing on earth was so wonderful as to be going home.

Already the African landscape looked a trifle thin, as though we were remembering rather than seeing it, and as the vehicles ground their way out over the mealie-field and I took my last look at Nyabánga, I could not grieve that I should never see it again. It had defeated us, as it had defeated Russell.

Though our pockets were light, I did not feel empty-handed. There are satisfactions which, if not as durable or as saleable as diamonds, are worth having; and in these I felt rich, though I could not have said for the life of me what they were. Instead of the calabash of diamonds, which had for so long obsessed us, we were leaving Mozambique with a fledgling pigeon and a pot of wild honey. The pigeon went to live with Michael in Salisbury, and the honey has long since been eaten; but I still have the pot and the shard.

Besides, there is a residue; the unlikely débris of an ambiguous experience; and I sometimes hear the echo of Umzila's laughter.